NICARAGUA AND THE UNITED STATES

NICARAGUA AND THE UNITED STATES
Years of Conflict

Tony Jenkins

Franklin Watts / New York / London / Toronto / Sydney / 1989

Map by Joe LeMonnier

Photographs courtesy of: INH/
Nueva Imagen: pp. 11, 20, 30, 35, 43, 50, 55,
57, 67; Paolo Bosio: pp. 79, 85, 89, 103, 117, 119,
124, 132, 138, 142, 143, 148, 158, 161, 164.

Library of Congress Cataloging-in-Publication Data

Jenkins, Tony.
Nicaragua and the United States; years of conflict / by Tony Jenkins.
p.   cm.
Bibliography: p.
Includes index.
Summary: Traces the history of the relationship between Nicaragua and the United States, from the nineteenth century to the present.
ISBN 0-531-10795-7
1. United States—Foreign relations—Nicaragua—Juvenile literature. 2. Nicaragua—Foreign relations—United States—Juvenile literature. [1. United States—Foreign relations—Nicaragua. 2. Nicaragua—Foreign relations—United States.]
I. Title.
E183.8.N5J46   1989
327.7285073—dc20   89-5758   CIP   AC

Copyright © 1989 by Tony Jenkins
All rights reserved
Printed in the United States of America
5 4 3 2 1

CONTENTS

Chapter One
First Encounters
/ 7 /

Chapter Two
A Few Hints for Al Capone
/ 14 /

Chapter Three
"That Damned Country"
/ 34 /

Chapter Four
The Somoza Dynasty and the
Triumph of the Sandinistas
/ 49 /

Chapter Five
The Honeymoon
/ 71 /

Chapter Six
The Divorce
/ 86 /

Chapter Seven
The Birth of the Contras
/ 99 /

Chapter Eight
Human Rights
/ 110 /

Chapter Nine
The Economy
/ 123 /

Chapter Ten
Holy War
/ 141 /

Chapter Eleven
From Reagan to Bush
/ 154 /

Chronology of
Dates in
Nicaraguan History / 172

Dictionary of
Acronyms Used in
This Book / 175

Notes / 177

For Further Reading / 187

Index / 188

NICARAGUA
AND THE
UNITED STATES

ONE

FIRST ENCOUNTERS

On January 24, 1848, James W. Marshall discovered gold at Sutter's Mill near what is now Sacramento, California. The discovery led to profound changes in the United States, and by a strange twist of geography and history, heralded the start of a long and bitter relationship between the U.S. and a small Spanish-speaking nation 3,000 miles to the south: Nicaragua.

News of Marshall's find sparked the Gold Rush.[1] Within two years 40,000 prospectors had made their way to the Pacific coast, and in their wake, over the next twenty years, followed half a million settlers. It was the last great pioneering wave which helped draw the map of the United States. But at first the trip west was fraught with problems. The transcontinental railroad would not be completed until 1869. In the meantime the overland route by wagon train took months and was plagued by Indian attacks which did not end until the Apache chief, Geronimo, surrendered in 1886.[2] The sea voyage was almost as long and the passage around Cape Horn was dangerous. The Panama Canal had not yet been built; in its place the canoe trip up the Chagres River, followed by mule train across the isthmus to Panama

City, was crowded and the route was infested with tropical diseases.[3]

As the early adventurers pored over their maps, they quickly discovered that the fastest safe way to reach California from the American east coast was through Nicaragua; it was the first time that many Americans had even heard of the country. The profit potential in this route caught the eye of Cornelius Vanderbilt, a self-made millionaire known as the "Commodore."[4] In 1849, at the head of a group of Wall Street investors, the Commodore persuaded the Nicaraguan government to grant him the rights to operate a ferry service and to build a canal.

Vanderbilt's Accessory Transit Company was launched into service with a fanfare of publicity in 1851. His ships shuttled between New York, New Orleans, and San Juan del Norte on Nicaragua's east coast. There passengers switched to shallow-draft paddle-boats which steamed up the beautiful Río San Juan and across Lake Nicaragua. On the west side of the lake, they transferred to stagecoaches to cover the dozen or so miles to the port of San Juan del Sur on the Pacific coast, where they once again boarded ships which took them to California.

Despite shipwrecks and miserable conditions the company established a reputation for speed, and passengers flocked to the Nicaraguan route. At one point as many as 2,000 a month were using the crossing, and the Commodore soon made a second fortune. However in 1853, while Vanderbilt was vacationing on his luxury yacht in the Mediterranean, two of his partners, Cornelius Garrison and Charles Morgan, seized control of the Accessory Transit Company. The Commodore sent them a furious note, "Gentlemen: You have undertaken to cheat me. I won't sue you, for the law is too slow. I'll ruin you. Yours truly, Cornelius Vanderbilt."[5]

The Walker Episode

In 1853 a civil war broke out in Nicaragua between the Liberal and the Conservative parties. Each side press-

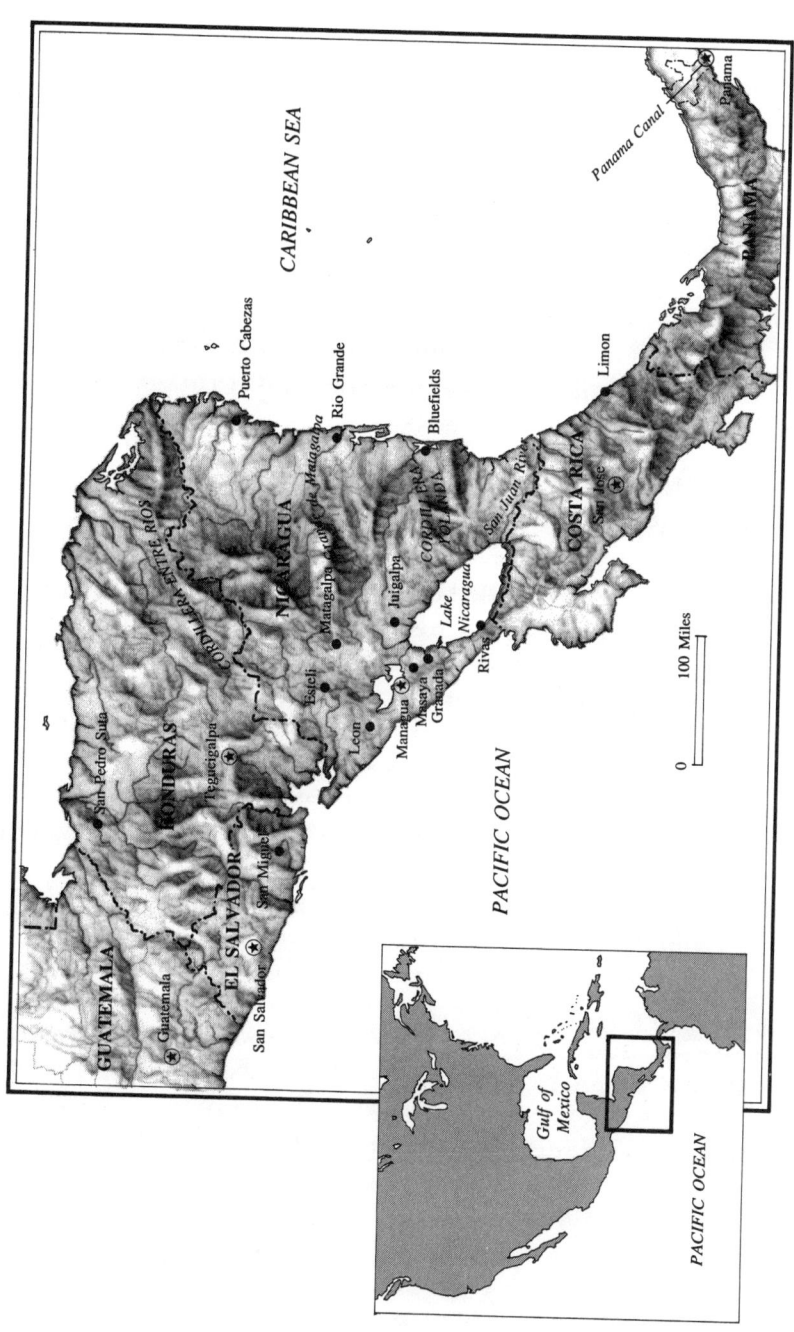

ganged untrained and badly equipped Nicaraguan peasants into their armies, but the Liberals hit upon the idea of recruiting experienced gunmen from the U.S. to do their fighting for them. The man hired to lead this force of desperadoes was an adventurer from Tennessee called William Walker.

A man who had worn many hats—doctor, lawyer, and journalist—Walker had acquired a national reputation when he started a private war in an unsuccessful bid to capture another piece of Mexican territory for the United States, five years after the two countries had settled the Mexican War. As his fame grew he came to be known in the U.S. as "the gray-eyed man of destiny."

It was a time when the frontiers of the U.S. were being rapidly expanded: Texas was annexed in 1845; the area that now comprises Idaho, Oregon, and Washington was acquired from the British in 1846; California, Nevada, Utah, New Mexico, Arizona, and parts of Colorado were seized or purchased from Mexico in 1848. To many Americans it seemed that theirs was a superior civilization that had a right and a duty to continue expanding throughout the Western Hemisphere, and Walker was popular for the way in which he seemed to embody this "manifest destiny" of the United States to conquer and "civilize" all of the Americas. In this context a private military expedition into Central America seemed perfectly reasonable to him. Walker recruited what he called a "Phalanx of Immortals"—56 mercenaries, better known in those days as filibusters—and set sail for Nicaragua from San Francisco in 1855.[6]

The filibusters quickly captured the Conservative stronghold of Granada, and Walker was appointed commander-in-chief of the army, but he had a bigger prize in mind. He plotted with Garrison and Morgan, who suspected that Vanderbilt would soon win back control of the Accessory Transit Company in a boardroom struggle. For his part of the deal Walker seized all the company assets and gave them to his new backers. In return they sent more than a thousand fresh American recruits to Nicaragua, with a

William Walker, the "gray-eyed man of destiny," attempted to forge the five Central American states into a single slave nation. In 1856 he proclaimed himself president of Nicaragua.

promise to send more to help colonize the country with white settlers, and they advanced him a large cash loan. With this support, in July 1856, Walker declared himself president.

But Walker's ambitions went still further than the presidency of Nicaragua. He was a fervent supporter of slavery: "The labor of the inferior races cannot compete with that of the white race unless you give it a white master to direct its energies," he wrote. "Without such protection as slavery affords, the colored races must inevitably succumb in the struggle with white labour."[7] He could see the United States slipping toward civil war and he dreamed of conquering all five Central American republics and demonstrating to abolitionists the superiority of a nation built on bondage.

Since 1847 the U.S. had been torn by a bitter political debate: on one side was the "Free-Soil" party, which opposed extending slavery into the new territories acquired during the Mexican War; on the other were the plantation owners and their supporters in the South.

To avoid a clear decision which might have led to the secession of the southern states, in 1854 Congress had passed the Kansas-Nebraska Act. It was a compromise which allowed the settlers of those two new territories to decide whether or not to permit slavery within their borders. The act caused both the pro-slavery and abolitionist forces to launch a furious effort to influence the outcome of the popular decision in Kansas, and Walker's action was part of that effort; if he could create new American-ruled slave states in Central America, he might be able to preempt the whole debate. He ordered his gunmen to embroider their flags with the motto "Five or None"—a reference to the five Central American republics; he reintroduced slavery, which had effectively been abolished by the Nicaraguan Constitution of 1826; and he declared English the official language.

To the horror of other Latin American leaders, President Franklin Pierce in Washington immediately recognized Walker's government and established diplomatic relations. The British were also alarmed at the prospect of filibuster-inspired U.S. expansionism in Central America; they thought it threatened their sugar colonies in the Caribbean, and they feared it could lead to a U.S. monopoly over the proposed canal, so they quietly let it be known that they would support a regional effort to evict the "Immortals." At the same time Vanderbilt paid his agents to whip up public feeling against Walker among Nicaragua's neighbors, and he offered to help finance a military operation. By December 1856 a combined army from El Salvador, Honduras, and Guatemala had forced Walker to retreat from Granada to Rivas, where a Costa Rican force joined the siege.

Meanwhile the British stationed a small fleet of warships off the Atlantic coast to discourage Washington, D.C. from coming to Walker's aid. Vanderbilt seized the moment to deliver the knockout blow. He paid a Costa Rican force to capture the river steamers that Walker was using for reinforcements and supplies. Starved of food and ammunition, the "Immortals" were forced to surrender, and on May 1, 1857, under the protection of a detachment of U.S. Marines, "President" Walker and his remaining followers boarded a ship and fled into exile.

When he reached the United States, Walker was given a hero's welcome and toured the country to widespread acclaim. This encouraged him to try again. He made two more expeditions to Central America, but eventually he was captured by the British, who handed him to the Honduran authorities: on September 12, 1860, the "gray-eyed man of destiny" was executed.

Behind him Walker left the nation's biggest city at the time, Granada, in ruins; as they retreated, his men had hung a sign on the waterfront which proclaimed "Here was Granada." Much of the Nicaraguan countryside was also devastated, and thousands died in a cholera epidemic caused by infections from the rotting corpses of the war victims. Nicaragua's first contact with the United States had not been a happy one.

TWO

A FEW HINTS FOR AL CAPONE

Walker's foray was not the first time Nicaragua had been ravaged by foreigners. The Spanish *conquistadores* led by Gil González de Avila had first invaded in 1522. The fertile plains of western Nicaragua were then inhabited by Chorotec Indians related to the Aztecs to the north.[1] Under the brave command of Diriangen, the Chorotecs bitterly resisted the attackers. They were considered such good warriors that after their defeat thousands were loaded into ships and sent south to help the Spaniards with the conquest of Peru; entire Indian towns were wiped out. The newly conquered territory was named after the local Indian chief, Nicarao, and it became a province of the colony of Guatemala, under the nominal rule of a viceroy appointed by the Spanish king.

Bartolomeo de las Casas, a Catholic bishop of the time, described the Chorotecs as healthy, cheerful, and prosperous. He said they cultivated beautiful orchards and were peaceful by nature until the *conquistadores* "subjected this people to so much evil, butchery, cruelty, bondage and injustice that no human tongue can describe it. . . . Today (1542) there must be four or five thousand persons in the whole of

Nicaragua. The Spaniards kill more every day through the services they exact and the daily personal oppression they exercise. And this ... used to be one of the most highly populated provinces in the world."[2]

The conquerors evicted the Chorotecs from their lands along the Pacific coast and established huge estates, which eventually came to be known as *haciendas*. The Indians were forced to work herding cattle, cutting timber, and producing vegetable dies and cocoa for export to other Latin American colonies and to Spain. However, until the nineteenth century, trade was often interrupted by pirate raids, war in Europe, and losses from storms at sea, and the region essentially lived an autonomous, self-sustained existence. In their spare time the Indians were permitted to cultivate some land which their communities farmed collectively, but theirs was a brutalized and hazardous existence: the lords of the *haciendas* effectively exercised absolute power, and as many as 400,000 Indians were sold to South America as slaves.[3]

Colonial Nicaragua, like all parts of the Spanish empire, was a rigidly hierarchical society. The kings' representatives at the top of the social pyramid lived in a luxurious cocoon, far removed from the misery of the peasants. The owners of large estates and aristocrats were treated with respect for their status and wealth, but there was no Bill of Rights and no hint of democracy. As late as 1600 there were only about 500 Spaniards in Nicaragua, lording it over some 150,000 Indians.

Until long after independence the vast majority of the population continued to be made up of Indians and *mestizos*—people of mixed Indian and European blood—who were equally disdained by the white colonial elite. Both groups eked a poor living off the land, the Indians in their collectives and the *mestizos* on their family allotments. In both cases the land often belonged to the lords of the estates, who would demand labor in return for the right to farm it. To escape these demands some Indians moved into the highlands and established new communities in what had once been virgin forest.

Independence

This semi-feudal system continued with little change for some 300 years. Then in 1808 Napoleon Bonaparte occupied Spain and deposed the Bourbon royal family. Nationalists in South America seized the opportunity to declare independence and finally defeated the Spanish forces in 1819. In 1821 Central America followed the southern continent's example. Tired of war, the government in Madrid offered no resistance, but within five months the new republics in the region were annexed by Emperor Iturbide of Mexico. After Iturbide was deposed and exiled, the five nations petitioned Washington, D.C., to join the United States. When that idea was rejected, they briefly formed the "United Provinces of Central America." The short-lived federation collapsed in 1839, at which point Nicaragua finally achieved complete independence.

But already the fledgling nation was deeply divided and riven by violence as two political parties competed for domination. As in most of Latin America, liberals and conservatives vied for control. But in Nicaragua politics were a function of geography. For more than two centuries the two biggest colonial cities had been León and Granada. León near the Pacific coast used the port of El Realejo to trade with other Spanish colonies. Granada, on the shores of the Gran Lago, or Great Lake, used the San Juan River to reach the Atlantic and to send its products to the motherland. Each city controlled its surrounding countryside and lived a virtually autonomous existence. For more than two centuries there were few links between them, and they evolved into virtual city-states inhabited by competing clans.

When politics started to play a role, around the time of independence, each city became the headquarters for a competing political party: León for the Liberals; Granada for the Conservatives. Most people chose their allegiance on the basis of geography and clan loyalty rather than ideology. The rivalry between the parties was so bitter and passionate that it frequently superseded national interests; as late as 1929 the correspondent for the *New York Times*, Harold Norman Denny, was able to state that "a man of circumstance is a Liberal or a Conservative first, a Nicaraguan afterward."[4] This meant that on several occasions political leaders were happier to invite U.S. intervention than to allow their political opponents to hold power, despite the lessons of the Walker episode.

Unlike Europe, mid-nineteenth century Nicaragua was not industrialized. No large concentrations of industrial workers existed to press for liberal social and political reforms. Both the Indians and *mestizos* were essentially agricultural workers, isolated in small groups throughout the Nicaraguan countryside, and they had little scope for political organizing. Between the mass of peasants and the handful of wealthy landowners, the middle class was tiny and politically insignificant.

Nevertheless the political struggle did contain elements of class and ideological differences. Many of the Conservatives were cattle barons, and some claimed descent from the *conquistadores*. They believed in an active political role for the Catholic Church and—happy with their trade links to Spain—they had opposed independence. The Liberals tended to be smaller landowners and artisans. They were influenced by English ideas of free trade and were unhappy with Church involvement in government. They wanted to cut all ties to Spain and to establish new markets. Their republicanism had been stirred by the French revolution and the American War of Independence.

Politics was a game for the elite, and the number of people who played was tiny. Neither the Indians nor the majority of *mestizos* were involved. For its first one hundred years of independence, despite a succession of high-sounding democratic constitutions, Nicaragua was effectively ruled by a squabbling elite. The philosophical differences between the two sides were often more apparent than real. In the end the competition was about something far more tangible than ideology: at independence the two cities fought to become the nation's capital, hoping to control such matters as taxation, land distribution, trade policy, and government patronage.

Between 1824 and 1842 Nicaragua witnessed seventeen major battles and eighteen different rulers, although the Liberals were almost consistently in control. Finally in 1845, with help from conservative governments in El Salvador and Honduras, the Conservatives managed to seize power and transferred the capital to Masaya, near Granada. In 1851 a Conservative general, Laureano Pineda, moved the capital to the small town of Managua, halfway between the two cities, in an effort to end the rivalry. It did not work. As we have seen, in their effort to grab power the Liberals hired William Walker. His defeat, and the destruction his adventure caused, so discredited the Liberals that they accepted Conservative rule for the next thirty-six years. Despite uprisings and coup attempts, it proved to be a relatively peaceful period in Nicaragua's history.

Cursed by Geography

The country that Walker had briefly made his personal fiefdom, and over which the Liberals and Conservatives so readily shed the peasants' blood, is approximately the size of North Carolina. It lies well to the south of the Tropic of Cancer and has two seasons: wet and dry. The rainy season lasts, roughly, from May to October.

A narrow fertile plain on the Pacific coast is dotted with a string of spectacular conical volcanoes whose occasional eruptions spew out the mineral-rich ash that makes the soil so productive. At its widest point the western plain stretches for about fifty miles. The combination of rich soil, abundant rain, and a long, hot, dry season make the west coast ideal for sugar and cotton plantations.

The Pacific plain is bounded to the northeast by a chain of highlands, known as the Darien Ridge, which contains small deposits of gold and silver. The highest point is nearly 7,000 feet. Because of their altitude the highlands escape the searing heat of the Nicaraguan dry season, which on the plains can send temperatures soaring into the nineties for days at a stretch.

On the slopes of the mountains are stands of deciduous trees. On the Atlantic side these break into tropical rain forest, then savannah and swamps. These features constitute a natural barrier that, until recently, isolated the Atlantic coast from the main power centers in the west.[5] The foothills of the Darien Ridge have been largely cleared of trees; the rolling land, particularly north and east of the Gran Lago, is excellent cattle country, which is why beef, hides, and tallow were the principal exports throughout the colonial period. Beef is still a major export. Together with coffee and cotton it accounts for 75 percent of Nicaragua's current foreign earnings, most of the rest coming from sugar, shellfish, bananas, and gold.

Although Nicaragua's agricultural and mineral wealth have yet to be fully exploited, it is the country's strategic location and topography that have made it the target of foreign interest. The Gran Lago, just 105 feet above sea level, and the San Juan River which it feeds, caused Nicaragua to be for many years the preferred location for the proposed interoceanic canal that was eventually built in Panama. Even the Spaniards dreamed of connecting the two seas through Nicaragua and marked the route on their maps as an *estrecho dudoso* or "possible pass."[6]

Later the British had the same ambition and exploited the isolation of the Caribbean coast to establish a "protectorate" among the Miskito Indians, whom they encouraged to attack the Spaniards. After the Spanish withdrawal the British had hopes of becoming the dominant colonial power in the region, and in 1848 they seized San Juan del Norte—or Greytown as it was then known—at the mouth of the Río San Juan and ran up the Miskito flag. The French too were mesmerized by the prospect of a canal through Nicaragua,

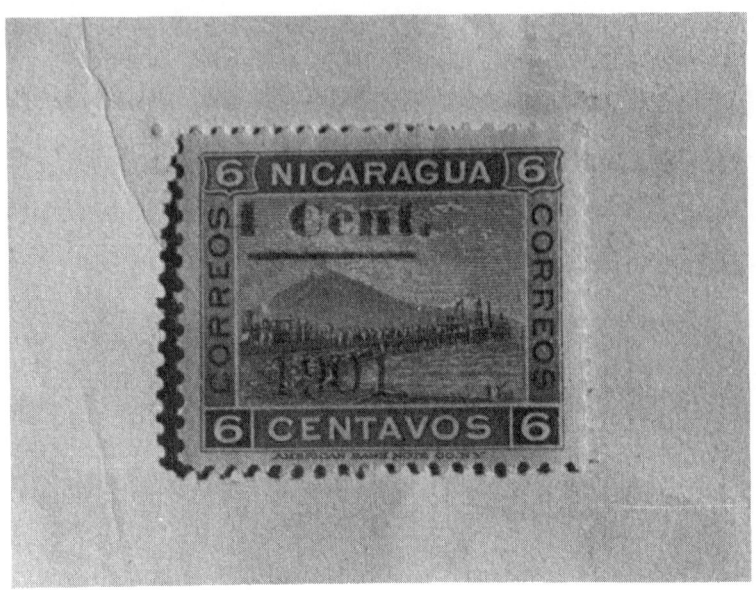

Nicaraguan postage stamp showing volcano on the shores of Lake Nicaragua. Opponents of the transisthmian canal proposed for Nicaragua distributed this stamp to members of the United States Congress. The canal was eventually built in Panama.

and Emperor Napoleon III, who established a brief puppet regime in Mexico from 1864 to 1867, compared Nicaragua's strategic location and potential wealth to the glories of Constantinople at the mouth of the Bosporus,[7] the waterway linking the Mediterranean and the Black Sea.

These European pretensions were vigorously opposed by the United States, which in those days still felt extremely vulnerable to pressure and competition from the old colonial powers—after all, as recently as 1814 the British had captured Washington, D.C., and burned down the White House. When Spain lost its colonies in Latin America, President James Monroe seized the opportunity to warn the European powers to forget any new colonial ambitions in the Western Hemisphere. In a speech to Congress in 1823, he announced his famous Monroe Doctrine that the U.S. would oppose any European interference in the Americas. At the time it was not interpreted as heralding U.S. imperialism in the region, and Latin Americans welcomed the speech.

Nevertheless in 1850 the canal-builders' ambitions were formalized when London and Washington signed the Clayton-Bulwer Treaty. It stipulated that any future canal through Nicaragua would be under joint British and U.S. control and that the two countries would split the tolls equally. The Nicaraguan government was not even consulted during the treaty negotiations.[8]

But as California started to develop and U.S. trading power grew, successive administrations came to realize the enormous benefits of a canal under exclusive U.S. control. It would not only help open up America's Pacific coast, it would cut the costs of trading with Latin America and help trade between the east coast and the Far East. When the canal was eventually built in Panama it became, in *New York Times* correspondent Denny's words, "part of the U.S. coastline... The United States could allow no other powerful country to establish a position of dominant influence between the Southern border and the canal." As one U.S. secretary of war, Henry Stimson, was later to admit, "It is of vital importance to this country not only that the canal should be open to *our* fleet in case of war, but that it should be closed to the fleet of our enemy."[9] This attitude was to become a major factor to U.S. intervention in Nicaragua.

King Coffee

It was, however, another aspect of geography that once again plunged Nicaragua into turmoil. During the nineteenth century a new fashion swept Europe and the United

States: coffee drinking. While the other Central American republics had been quick to take advantage of this trend, Nicaragua's constant internecine warfare distracted landowners from the fortune that could be made from the "green gold." The combination of moderately warm temperatures, high rainfall, and rich soil make Nicaragua's northern highlands ideal for cultivating coffee. By the 1880s the Indians were once again being evicted from what was left of the communal lands they had farmed for generations. Huge new estates were carved out of the highland communities they had established to escape earlier evictions by the cattle barons. And, because coffee cultivation is a much more labor-intensive operation than cattle-rearing, the laws banning forced labor were altered, making it much easier once again to compel Indians to work. As in other parts of Central America, there was a brief Indian uprising to protest this fresh bout of exploitation. It was swiftly and ruthlessly put down and thousands were slaughtered.

Yet for the Liberals the changes came too slowly. They suspected that the Conservatives were more interested in cattle ranching than in helping the growing new class of Liberal entrepreneurs who were expanding Nicaragua's coffee exports. They were convinced that they were better prepared to harness the new trade boom and its demands for a vigorous government to modernize infrastructure, such as roads and ports. And they chafed with impatience as the Conservatives slowly conducted the business of government from the secluded patios of their mansions in Granada. Finally the Liberals could stand it no longer. Led by General José Santos Zelaya, in 1893 they staged a rebellion and seized power.

The Liberal Dictatorship

Zelaya was a dynamic and ruthless modernizer. He built roads, railways, ports, and telegraph lines. He established public education and a government bureaucracy. His army became the best trained and equipped in Central America, and he used it to install a friendly Liberal regime in neighboring Honduras. Zelaya also had ambitions to extend his influence throughout Central America and almost succeeded in establishing a regional confederation. In 1895, with U.S. diplomatic backing, he ousted the British from the east coast and, for the first time, united Nicaragua under one government. However Zelaya's modernizing fervor did not extend to the institutions of democracy. He maintained his sixteen-year hold on power through a series of farcical elections; according to one account voters were once given a choice of three candidates: "José, Santos, or Zelaya."[10]

Zelaya was also corrupt. He sold "concessions" to American companies to exploit Nicaragua's natural resources and pocketed the money for himself. For example, he sold huge tracts of land to a U.S. timber concern called the Bragman's Bluff Lumber Company. He sold the rights to mine for gold to La Luz and Los Angeles Mining Company. He even sold the exclusive rights to navigate on certain rivers and a monopoly to sell liquor throughout the country. It marked the start of major U.S. investment in Nicaragua.

Banana Republics

The largest American investment of this period was to start a little later, in 1921: it was made by the Standard Fruit Company. Nicaragua's tropical climate and the high rainfall on the palm- and mangrove-lined Caribbean coast make it an ideal location for banana plantations. Throughout Central America, Standard Fruit and its great rival United Fruit established huge estates, employing thousands of people. The companies came to wield enormous influence, starting wars and making and breaking governments. Even as late as 1954 United Fruit helped to depose the elected president of Guatemala.

For this and other reasons the benefits of U.S. investment were questionable. They brought employment and above-average wages, some local medical care, roads, railways, and telephone lines, but the effects were highly localized and often short-lived. The railways, for example, were designed solely to link plantations to ports. Thus, although the Caribbean coast of Honduras has hundreds of miles of track, the nation's inland capital, Tegucigalpa, is not connected to the railway system. In addition the workers were often paid in "scrip"—company vouchers that could only be spent in company stores.

In 1929 Denny wrote that Puerto Cabezas on Nicaragua's Caribbean coast "is operated like a tiny principality by the Standard Fruit Company... This American company owns the town and everything in it."[11] He said American families rented company houses, bought their clothes and food in company stores, and relaxed in the company club, leaving little scope for local businessmen. It seems highly symbolic that when Standard Fruit eventually pulled out of Puerto Cabezas it ripped up the railway line and sold the steel. Today it is difficult to find any evidence of the company's former presence.[12]

The American investments brought with them hundreds of American workers and businessmen. In times of unrest this often led to the dispatch of American troops to protect American property and lives. However, that justifiable concern would also be used throughout the region on numerous occasions as a pretext for military intervention in order to establish governments sympathetic to the United States.

The Big Stick

The birth of this imperial period in the history of the United States was marked by President Theodore Roosevelt's occupancy of the White House. Roosevelt was convinced that "superior" nations had the right and the duty to dominate "inferior" ones in the interests of civilization. He believed that a widespread empire was the sign of greatness, and was anxious that the U.S. should have one of its own. For that reason he was determined to prevent any European meddling in Latin America that might undermine U.S. dominance. In particular Roosevelt was anxious to forestall European action when several countries in the region defaulted on railroad construction loans borrowed from European banks. That was the reason he moved quickly to secure American-controlled debt collection in the Dominican Republic in 1904, before the Europeans sent gunboats themselves. Fear of European financial involvement was also to motivate Roosevelt in his policy toward Nicaragua.

In 1904 Roosevelt announced his "corollary" to the Monroe Doctrine: "Chronic wrongdoing or an impotence which results in a general loosening of the ties of civilized society may, in America as elsewhere, ultimately require intervention by some civilized nation, and in the Western Hemisphere the adherence of the United States to the Monroe Doctrine may force the United States, however reluctantly, in flagrant cases of such wrongdoing or impotence to the exercise of an international police power." Roosevelt firmly believed in this international duty, but to others such intervention was merely self-interest masquerading as a moral obligation.

Another tenet of Roosevelt's grandiose personal philosophy was that the best way to establish U.S. dominance was on the battlefield. "No triumph of peace is quite so great as the supreme triumph of war," he said. As assistant secretary of the navy in 1898 he helped propel the U.S. into war with Spain over Cuba—which also led to the acquisition of Puerto Rico and the Philippines. In 1903, as president, Roosevelt engineered the independence of Panama from Colombia so that the canal could be built on U.S. terms; as he later boasted, "I took Panama." He sent troops to Puerto Cortes in Honduras in 1905 and to Panama in 1908. Marines were also dispatched to occupy Cuba between 1906 and 1909. Besides the "chronic wrongdoing" which demanded the U.S. presence, Cuba and Puerto Rico also had the advantages of controlling the principal Caribbean sea routes to the canal. The policy of using U.S. Marines to advance American interests became known as the policy of the Big Stick.

Nicaragua was to become one of the first victims of the Big Stick. The problems started in 1903 when Zelaya suffered a major setback. He had counted on the transisthmian canal being built through Nicaragua to provide the impetus for fresh economic growth and development. When the U.S. decided instead to build the canal in Panama, relations between Washington and Managua quickly deteriorated. Zelaya approached Britain and Japan to build a rival canal, an idea which Roosevelt viewed with deep suspicion.

Despite the announcement of the corollary, in 1907 Zelaya made clear his expansionist intentions by invading Honduras and rapidly defeating armies from that country and from El Salvador. It was an irritation Roosevelt could do without; he summoned representatives from all five Central American countries to Washington and ordered them to settle their differences. Finally in 1908 the troublesomely independent Zelaya went too far. He cancelled some U.S. business concessions and negotiated a major loan with a British financial syndicate, despite warnings from the U.S. secretary of state that such a move would violate the Monroe Doctrine. Washington was now ready to help nudge Zelaya from power.

In 1909 events came to a head. The dissident Liberal governor of the Caribbean town of Bluefields, Juan Estrada, launched a rebellion backed by leading Conservatives including Adolfo Díaz, who was the secretary of the American-owned Luz and Los Angeles Mining Company. The legal adviser to the company was the U.S. secretary of state, Philander C. Knox. It was clear that, at the very least, Estrada had Knox's tacit approval, and at his request 400 marines landed in Bluefields under the pretext of protecting U.S. property and lives.[13] In the first battle Estrada was badly beaten by Zelaya's men; he fell back to Bluefields and the cover of the U.S. troops.

In desperation the rebels hired two Americans to sabotage Zelaya's troop ships. The men were captured, summarily tried, and executed. At last Knox had an excuse to act. In Washington the cabinet considered invading Nicaragua, but settled instead for breaking diplomatic relations and demanding an indemnity. In a curt note to Zelaya, Knox hinted that the repercussions would be less severe if a new government were installed in Managua. Having witnessed the U.S. interventions in Cuba, Puerto Rico, Panama, and Honduras, Zelaya knew the threat was not an empty one. He resigned after declaring that he hoped to remove the "pretext" for further U.S. intervention. His wish was not to be granted.[14]

Zelaya's successor, Dr. José Madriz, was another Liberal. Although he had a reputation for being both honest and capable, Madriz was unacceptable to Knox, who was determined to install a totally new and more pliant administration in Managua. The fighting resumed, and backed by the threat of U.S. intervention, Estrada was able to defeat the government forces.

To ensure that the new government would be amenable to U.S. interests, the State Department hurriedly sent an envoy, Thomas Dawson, to negotiate a pact. Dawson decided elections would be destabilizing. They were postponed, and Estrada was allowed to rule for two years. More importantly, Estrada agreed not to stand in the next elections and to appoint Díaz as his vice president (Díaz was obviously being groomed for the presidency). After this scheme was approved by the State Department, an un-elected Constituent Assembly dutifully "elected" Estrada and Díaz on the last day of 1910.[15]

As part of the Dawson pact, Estrada agreed to restore the U.S. concessions and to borrow money from U.S. banks to pay off the British loans that Zelaya had contracted. As a guarantee to creditors, the Nicaraguan national bank, tax collection service, customs department, and railways were placed under the control of two New York banks, W. Seligman & Co. and Brown Brothers & Co. The bankers promised to build a railway from the east coast to the west; it never materialized. Meanwhile both banks made large profits from the deal. In 1929 Denny wrote, "The United States has ruled Nicaragua during most of the past 18 years more completely than the American Federal Government rules any state in the Union."[16] Some congressmen justified this interference as helping the Nicaraguans to resolve their financial problems and claimed that the U.S. presence brought other advantages such as structural developments. Apart from some improvements to the railways—designed to boost their profitability for the bankers—this was not the case. Indeed, commenting on the Zelaya period, Denny said "a better educational system was maintained then than the feeble one existing today."[17]

The U.S. Occupation

The small clique of party leaders who negotiated with Dawson were not able to adhere to the terms of the pact for long. Within five months Estrada had been pushed from office and Díaz took over. Díaz was weak; both he and his rivals knew it. In a desperate search for protection he wrote to the U.S. Embassy proposing a treaty and an amendment to the Nicaraguan constitution "permitting the United States to intervene in our internal affairs in order to maintain peace."[18] The suggestion was rejected: Roosevelt's successor, President William Howard Taft, wanted to replace the Big Stick with what one historian has called "Dollar Diplomacy." Taft hoped to extend U.S. influence through commerce rather than force. Nevertheless Taft's ambitions were as extravagant as those of his predecessor. On one occasion the president boasted, "The day is not far distant when three

Stars and Stripes at three equidistant points will mark our territory: one at the North Pole, another at the Panama Canal and the third at the South Pole. The whole Hemisphere will be ours in fact as, by virtue of our superiority of race, it is already ours morally."[19]

Yet within 14 months Díaz faced a rebellion and felt obliged to turn to his benefactors in Washington for help. On August 4, 1912, a detachment of American sailors landed, followed by a force of 2,700 marines under the command of Major Smedley D. Butler. The marines routed the rebels and captured their leader, the Liberal hero General Benjamin Zeledon, who was later declared to have "died in battle."[20] Zeledon's decapitated corpse was paraded through Nicaraguan towns and villages as an example. From then until 1933—except for one brief twelve-month period from 1925 to 1926—Nicaragua was continuously occupied by American troops, longer than any other country in the hemisphere.

However Nicaragua was far from unique. Presidents Woodrow Wilson, Warren Harding, Calvin Coolidge and Herbert Hoover diligently followed the example of their predecessors. "Police actions" and occupations by the United States throughout the period took place in Honduras (1910, 1912, 1919, 1924); Panama (1912, 1918); Haiti (1914 to 1934); Dominican Republic (1916 to 1924); and Cuba (1917 to 1923).

In Nicaragua the American presence was widely welcomed by the elite. As one Conservative politician asked in a speech before the Hall of Deputies in 1916, "What would become of us if our little nation did not have a great nation like the United States to restrain us from our mistakes? Intervention by the United States is an absolute necessity."[21] Such comments would be remembered sixty years later by the revolutionaries who seized power; they would argue that the elite was not to be trusted because it had consistently sold out to U.S. interests.

A battalion of U.S. marines on parade in Managua. The marines were stationed in Nicaragua almost continuously between 1912 and 1933, the longest period of time U.S. forces have occupied another country in the Western Hemisphere.

Setting the Stage for Sandino

Although American diplomats occasionally talked about the need for free and fair elections in underdeveloped countries, their major concern was to ensure stability. In the case of Nicaragua that could best be achieved by allowing the Conservatives to retain power. So from 1912 to 1924 the presidency was passed around like a family heirloom. From Díaz it was bestowed on the most powerful Conservative general, Emiliano Chamorro, who handed it on to his uncle Diego Manuel Chamorro. All three men were unusually submissive to U.S. interests. In 1914, for example, Emiliano Chamorro, while ambassador to Washington, negotiated a treaty with U.S. Secretary of State William Jennings Bryan which granted permanent U.S. sovereignty over the entire proposed Nicaraguan canal route and the right to build two military bases on Nicaraguan soil. In exchange Nicaragua theoretically received $3 million, but the money was immediately paid to American bankers to cover old debts. Even by the standards of the period the treaty was a shameful invasion of Nicaraguan sovereignty, and for several years the U.S. Senate refused to ratify it.

The purpose of the agreement was not to benefit Nicaragua in any way, but to secure U.S. interests, to ensure "stability," and to prevent anyone from building a rival to the highly profitable and strategically vital Panama canal.[22] These concerns were to dominate U.S. policy until 1979 and were used to justify U.S. support for the bloody dictatorship which was to come. Few Americans expressed any regrets, but in 1935 Butler, by then a retired Marine Corps general, wrote, "I spent most of my time being a high-class muscle man for Big Business, for Wall Street and for the bankers. In short I was a racketeer for capitalism... I helped purify Nicaragua for the international banking house of Brown Brothers... I feel I might have given Al Capone a few hints."[23]

But in 1924 the subservient chain of command was broken when a group of dissident Conservatives, in an unusual coalition with the Liberals, won elections under a U.S.-imposed voting system, defeating General Chamorro's attempt to secure an unconstitutional second term. The new president was the Conservative Carlos Solorzano and the vice president was a Liberal, Juan Bautista Sacasa. Chamorro's response was to rebel. He quickly drove the Liberals out of government and took for himself the post of vice president. Then in 1926 he forced Solorzano to resign in his favor. The Liberals objected, claimed that the presidency had passed by default to Sacasa, and started an uprising on the Atlantic coast, which they called the "Constitutionalist War."

The revolt was quickly halted by U.S. troops, and leaders of both parties were invited aboard a U.S. warship where Washington's solution was announced: the faithful Adolfo Díaz was once again to be president. At the time President Coolidge admitted that his overriding concern was to protect American rights to build a canal in Nicaragua and a naval base on Nicaraguan soil in the Gulf of Fonseca.

By then the United States had become accustomed to obedience in Central America. As under secretary of state Robert Olds wrote in a memorandum in 1927, "Our Ministers accredited to the five little republics, stretching from the Mexican border to Panama, have been advisers whose advice has been accepted virtually as law in the capitals where they respectively reside... We do control the destinies of Central America and we do so for the simple reason that the national interest absolutely dictates such a course ... Until now Central America has always understood that governments which we recognize and support stay in power, while those we do not recognize and support fail."[24]

But Sacasa obviously did not understand the rules of the game. He rejected the proposed arrangement and established a rival government on the Atlantic coast. His minister of war, José María Moncada, launched a series of successful attacks which underlined the fragility of the Díaz regime. Sacasa's success was due in part to the support he received from President Plutarco Elias Calles of Mexico, who saw an opportunity to undermine U.S. influence in the region. For his part the U.S. secretary of state Frank B. Kellogg accused the Mexicans of being Bolsheviks and used this as an excuse to dispatch more troops and munitions to Díaz.[25] U.S. Marines quickly occupied the major towns on the Pacific coast and seized the railways and ports. The occupation caused protests throughout the world and even in Washington, where Senator Burton Wheeler said the policy of President Calvin Coolidge "has led to armed intervention in Nicaragua in behalf of an American-made puppet-President foisted upon the people against their own will for the simple reason that he is ready at whatever cost to Nicaragua to serve the New York bankers who for seventeen years have been mercilessly exploiting Nicaragua under the aegis of the State Department."[26]

Despite the presence of the marines, the Liberal army continued to advance rapidly on Managua. To stave off defeat, Coolidge dispatched the former secretary of war, Henry Stimson, with the authority to impose a solution. On May 4, 1927, Stimson met Moncada outside Managua in the shade of an *espino negro* or blackthorn tree. He offered Moncada two options: an immediate Liberal surrender, which would allow Díaz to complete his term until 1928 when fresh elections would be held under the supervision of U.S. Marines, or a fight against U.S. troops. To sweeten the deal the top Liberal officers were to be given well-paid government posts controlling six provinces, as well as farms and horses, and, it was hinted, Moncada would receive U.S. backing in the 1928 elections.[27] Moncada opted for the carrot instead of the stick. On May 12th he and all but one of his generals signed the peace terms, known as the Espino Negro Pact, and surrendered their weapons to the marines. The general was Augusto César Sandino.

THREE

"THAT DAMNED COUNTRY"

As President Coolidge's envoy, Stimson, packed his bags for Washington, he was informed that Sandino had last been seen heading north with just 200 men. He concluded that the lone rebel posed little threat, and he telegraphed the State Department that "the civil war in Nicaragua is now definitely ended." He recommended that the major tasks ahead should be to supervise the 1928 elections and to create a new, apolitical Nicaraguan army to be known as the Guardia Nacional (National Guard). Until then Nicaragua's armies had always owed their allegiance to one or another of the political parties, a system that fueled the cycle of civil war. Urged on by foreign businessmen who wanted to create a safe climate for their investments, Stimson was determined to break the pattern.

Sandino soon had even fewer troops. When he reached Jinotega in northern Nicaragua, he released all the men with family commitments; just forty remained. Nevertheless he cabled his defiance to Managua, called Moncada a traitor, and vowed to fight on. On May 18th he married a telegraph operator called Blanca Arauz, and three days later instead of honeymooning he disappeared into the mountains. But

Augusto Cesar Sandino (center), the liberal general who refused to surrender to the U.S. marines. His action inspired the Sandinista guerrillas who overthrew the Somoza dictatorship in 1979.

Sandino did not march off into oblivion. Within a year his name was making headlines around the world.

"The General of Free Men"

Stimson and his colleagues can be forgiven for having underestimated Sandino; he was the first Nicaraguan leader in more than twenty years who refused to be seduced by offers of power and money. The rest were like Moncada, who scoffed at Sandino: "How can you think of dying for the people? The people do not reward, the important thing is to live well."[1] But Sandino's background was different from that of most of his contemporaries on the Nicaraguan political stage.

Sandino was born in 1895 in the village of Niquinohomo, the illegitimate son of a rich grain merchant and an Indian field worker. Initially abandoned by his father, he had a miserable childhood; at the age of nine he watched his mother have a bloody miscarriage in a debtors' prison. When he reached eleven his father finally recognized him, sent him to school, and allowed him to live in the servants' quarters. Like most *mestizos* he was a short man and that, along with his early poverty, may have accounted for his lifelong shyness. Nevertheless, by the time he was twenty-five he had established his own successful grain business, and in 1920 he was about to marry his childhood sweetheart and settle into a simple life when his world collapsed. During a petty village quarrel he shot and wounded another man and fled the country to escape arrest.

For the next six years Sandino roamed around Central America and Mexico, working intermittently as a security guard for an American sugar company in Honduras, as a field hand on an American banana plantation in Guatemala, and as a mechanic and salesman for an American oil company in the Mexican port of Tampico. Although these experiences must have opened his eyes to the power wielded by U.S. corporations in Latin America, it was not until he encountered left-wing trade unionists in Mexico that Sandino had his first taste of anti-American nationalism. As he later liked to recall, he decided to return to Nicaragua following a political discussion in a bar in Tampico when one of his co-workers accused all Nicaraguans of being *vendepatrias,* people who sell out their country.[2] As soon as he returned he used his own savings to arm a small band of fighters. Under his intelligent leadership it quickly grew and scored some useful victories in Moncada's rebellion.

It was not ardent nationalism, though, that first inspired Sandino to reject the Espino Negro pact. What he resented was that by imposing the Díaz presidency, the constitution had once again been overturned to keep a Conservative in power. At first he even suggested that Nicaragua should be governed by a team of U.S. Marine officers until the 1928 elections.[3] But once it became obvious that Washington was going to help Díaz cling to power, he quickly turned against the *Yanqui agresor*. Latin American nationalists delightedly embraced him as a symbol of resistance to U.S. interference in the affairs of the continent: to many of them he became known as "The General of Free Men."[4]

"The Crazy Little Army"

On June 9th a detachment of U.S. Marines arrived in the northern garrison town of Ocotal. They were commanded by Captain Gilbert Hatfield, who hoped to persuade Sandino to surrender. For weeks the two men exchanged a bizarre series of telegraphed messages that became increasingly insulting. At one point an exasperated Hatfield wrote, "If words were bullets and phrases were soldiers, you would be a field marshal instead of a mule thief." Finally Sandino swore to expel all Americans from Nicaragua, and he wired Hatfield: "I will not surrender and I await you here. *Quiero patria libre o morir* [I want a free homeland or death]."

This was to become the slogan of his men, and a generation later it was adopted by the left-wing guerrillas who were inspired by his example and who called themselves Sandinistas. Sandino boasted to Hatfield, "I am not afraid of you. I count on the ardor of the patriotism of those who accompany me." He concluded with a promise to attack Ocotal, signing himself "Your most obedient servant who ardently desires to put you in a handsome tomb with beautiful bouquets of flowers."[5]

Hatfield received reinforcements from the newly formed Guardia Nacional, which marine officers were scrambling to shape into a credible fighting force. Nevertheless, on July 16th Sandino attacked Ocotal with 600 men—most of them Indians and peasants armed only with machetes—a ragtag band that inspired a paean from the Chilean poet, Gabriela Mistral, to "the crazy little army."

The defenders, barricaded in the town hall and adjacent barracks, kept up a withering hail of machine gun and rifle fire. Yet the battle raged for seventeen hours, until the marines used their surprise weapon: five De Havilland airplanes summoned by radio from Managua, which made the first recorded aerial dive-bombing raid in history and forced the attackers to retreat. Many of the Indians had never even seen a plane before, and Sandino said later that the noise alone had been enough to make them panic.[6]

After the battle, Hatfield claimed 300 of Sandino's men had been killed for the loss of one marine. Whether or not the figures were accurate, Sandino had learned the cost of attacking fixed positions, and for the next five and a half years he relied on guerrilla tactics: ambushes and lightning raids.

During that period Sandino built a formidable fighting force which he called the Army for the Defense of the National Sovereignty. It marched under his trademark red and black flag, and at its peak it had as many as 6,000 men divided into 21 columns that operated throughout the country. His army even included a detachment of foreign volunteers drawn from at least nine Latin American countries, a forerunner of the famous International Brigades of the Spanish Civil War.

As early as 1928 Sandino had formed what amounted to a provisional government in the large swaths of territory he intermittently controlled. Under military supervision his sympathizers minted their own currency from captured gold mines and ran a radio and telephone network with equipment seized from the marines. They raised taxes on large landowners and foreign companies, forcing them to adopt a progressive labor code and to pay unemployed workers. They set up classes to teach peasant soldiers to read and write, and most important of all, they distributed land and organized peasant cooperatives, which gave Sandino an insight into how to resolve the most explosive social issue in Nicaragua—the land question.

Since the arrival of the *conquistadores*, the Indians and *mestizos* had been confined to small parcels of land on which they could barely grow enough food to subsist. Their poverty ensured their willingness to accept poorly paid, backbreaking seasonal labor on the coffee and sugar estates. By establishing cooperatives on virgin land, Sandino believed the peasants could pool resources and ensure year-round work providing cereals and meat for the cities.[7]

Despite his impressive organization the marines continued to call Sandino and his men bandits, which prompted one U.S. senator to suggest that if the War Department was so keen on fighting bandits, it might be better off tackling Al Capone in Chicago.[8]

It is possible that some of Sandino's men were former bandits. If so he forced them to adopt a new regime: they went unpaid and were not allowed to loot. He himself scrupulously left signed vouchers undertaking to repay whatever food, ammunition, or livestock he "borrowed," unless it was from a foreign landowner. Sandino seems to have had a magnetic power to recruit volunteers; while he offered no detailed political program, his ringing speeches about social justice and an end to foreign oppression must have inspired the Indians, who could still remember the lands from which they had been evicted during the first coffee boom. The Great Depression boosted the rebel ranks. Falling exports threw many peasants out of work. By joining Sandino's army they were at least guaranteed food, and it must have been an appealing way for the unemployed to express their grievances.

Like all successful guerrillas, Sandino counted on widespread local support. He knew the terrain and spoke the language. The marines on the other hand found themselves in a foreign land, tramping through jungles and swamps, plagued by mosquitoes and strange diseases, constantly subject to surprise attack—they came to call Nicaragua "that damned country."9 Some even deserted and surrendered to Sandino's forces.

In an attempt to undermine support for Sandino, the marines and the U.S.-led Guardia forcibly relocated thousands of peasants, burned their crops, destroyed their houses, and in the "no-go" areas this policy created, they treated anyone found as a bandit. Several atrocities were committed by both sides, and a famous photograph of the period shows a marine brandishing the decapitated head of one of Sandino's men. Many of the dislodged peasants were forced into internment camps, where more than 200 starved to death. Entire villages were razed in dive-bombing attacks from the air. But such tactics only served to win more supporters for Sandino's cause.

Nicaragua was not the only country in the region to be wracked by conflict. Indeed the economic collapse of the 1930s led to uprisings throughout Central America. The largest of these was in El Salvador, where one of Sandino's senior aides, the Communist Farabundo Martí, led a revolt in 1932. It was brutally put down, and some 30,000 Indians and *mestizos* were massacred. Three U.S. warships—and two destroyers sent from Canada at Britain's request—patrolled the Salvadoran coast, ready to intervene if the rebellion slipped out of control.

In Nicaragua, however, besides sending growing numbers of troops, Washington also tried a political approach, organizing elections in 1928. With marines guarding the ballot boxes and an American general counting the votes, Moncada was declared president; Stimson had kept his word. The State Department had hoped that a Liberal president would be able to convince the guerrillas to surrender, but Sandino despised Moncada and refused to give up until all American troops left the country. His forces grew. He captured and destroyed American properties, such as the Luz and Los Angeles gold mines and the Standard Fruit Company's banana fields, several of whose American employees were massacred in 1931. By 1932 the two sides were fighting at least every other day, and Sandino's army listed 176 engagements in that year.[10] Remarkably, throughout all this combat only 122 marine and Guardia deaths were reported. Nevertheless they were enough to cause an extraordinary reaction, both in the U.S. and around the world.

In 1928 the International Conference of American States was dominated by the Nicaraguan situation to the embarrassment of President Calvin Coolidge. The Democrats seized the issue, making withdrawal from Nicaragua part of their 1928 election campaign platform. In 1929, during a vigorous fight in Congress, they almost succeeded in halting funds for the occupation. Marines posted for duty in Nicaragua were sent letters begging them to refuse to fight. Throughout the U.S. and Latin America solidarity committees were set up by the All-America Anti-Imperialist League. They organized demonstrations and sent Sandino money. The White House was picketed; demonstrators carried signs declaring "Wall Street and not Sandino is the *real* bandit." In Europe conferences were held to publicize his cause. Sandino's fame even extended as far as China, where troops of the Kuomingtang nationalist party brandished his portrait as they marched into Peking in 1928 during that country's long civil war. Some of the American press treated Sandino like a modern Robin Hood, a reputation that prompted the "king" of Hollywood, Cecil B. DeMille, to ask the State Department for permission to make a film about the little guerrilla hero from Nicaragua—the request was denied.

Faced with an unwinnable war and unrelenting bad publicity, the administration of President Herbert Hoover, which came to office in 1929, decided to expand the Guardia Nacional so that it could handle all combat duties and provide the marines with a plausible pretext for a dignified exit. In today's military jargon we would say the White House decided to "Nicaraguanize" the war. In 1932 a new round of elections was held under U.S. supervision. They were won by Juan Bautista Sacasa, the man for whom Sandino had first taken up arms. Heavy fighting continued, but as promised, on January 1, 1933, the last contingent of marines left Nicaragua.

Anastasio Somoza García

But the U.S. had one last important task to perform in Nicaragua before this chapter of history could be closed: a local leader had to be found for the Guardia Nacional. For five years Nicaragua's new national army had been commanded by a succession of American officers. At one point 205 of the 220 officers in the Guardia were simultaneously active-duty U.S. Marine officers. But President Hoover insisted on a total U.S. military withdrawal, and so, ready or not, a Nicaraguan had to take command. The man chosen, with strong backing from U.S. Ambassador Matthew Hanna but against the wishes of Sacasa, was Anastasio Somoza García, known to all by his nickname "Tacho."

Like Sandino, Somoza was born in a poor village and had spent part of his youth abroad, although his travels took him farther north to the United States, where he studied at a minor business school and worked as a toilet inspector and used-car salesman. Like Sandino, Somoza quickly joined the Liberal cause during the "Constitutionalist War," and despite the rapid defeat of his little band of men, he too awarded himself the title of general. But there the similarities ended. While Sandino made a virtue of being an underdog and took defiant and self-conscious pride in his lonely sacrifices in the mountains, Tacho boasted of his worldliness and his contacts with the powerful. From his wanderings Somoza had picked up fluent English, spiced with an earthy vocabulary that amused visiting American dignitaries such as Stimson, for whom he worked as an interpreter in 1927. From his great-uncle Bernabe Somoza—a notorious highway thief—he seems to have inherited charm and contempt for the law; in 1921 he had been arrested and tried for forging checks to pay off his

Anastasio Somoza Garcia, founder of a 40-year political dynasty in Nicaragua, cultivated good relations with the United States and amassed a personal fortune through corruption and theft.

gambling debts. He was wily, witty, and ingratiating. He married above himself, to Sacasa's niece Salvadora Debayle Sacasa before the old man became president. By 1932 he had served as minister of war and minister of foreign relations. At the same time, according to at least one account, he earned his Guardia appointment by becoming the lover of Ambassador Hanna's wife.[11]

Whatever the reason for his appointment as Jefe Director, Somoza was not content just to run the army. He was extremely ambitious and had every intention of using the Guardia as a power base from which to capture the presidency. But first he had to remove his biggest threat: Sandino.

"The Death of Caesar"

With the departure of the marines, Sandino's major demand had been met; he was now prepared to negotiate. On February 2nd he flew to Managua and was greeted at the airport by Tacho. The two embraced as old comrades-in-arms and drove together to the presidential palace while cheering crowds lined the route. Within hours a treaty was hammered out, and amid national rejoicing, peace was declared. Sandino agreed to disarm all but a hundred of his men, to be retained as a personal guard. In return he was given more than nine million acres of virgin land stretching from the northern mountains to the Atlantic coast, nearly a third of the entire country. For one year Sandino's men would be paid by the government to police this state-within-a-state, and some would be given jobs supervising a special government investment program in the north. But Sandino had no intention of joining Nicaragua's exclusive club of millionaire landowners. He dreamed instead of using the land to establish a string of voluntary peasant cooperatives, a sort of socialist utopia he hoped would provide a political example to the rest of the country that was still dominated by the huge estates of the Liberal and Conservative elite.

During more than six years of guerrilla war Sandino's views had become increasingly radical. Following the onset of the Great Depression in 1929, world coffee prices collapsed, Nicaraguan mines and lumber companies closed, and unemployed workers flocked to his army, introducing a conscious element of class conflict. It was fostered by the antagonism of the rich, who branded him a bandit and begged the marines for protection. The poor, on the other hand, gave Sandino's men food, shelter, and information. Sandino came to rely on them. At one point he declared "only the workers and peasants will see it through to the end."[12] On another occasion he warned "very soon we shall have our victory in Nicaragua and with it the fuse of the 'proletarian explosion' will be lit against the imperialists of the world."[13]

Sandino distrusted the traditional parties. He suspected that they would continue to encourage U.S. interference in Nicaraguan affairs for as long as they could make a quick buck out of it. His original peace terms stipulated an end to foreign intervention in the Guardia and demanded a Pan American conference to revise the humiliating Bryan-Chamorro canal treaty. In interviews with the local press, after the declaration of peace, he said that while he welcomed Americans generally, he rejected Americans who came to Nicaragua as bosses.[14] In early 1933, he approved the creation of a new nationalist party.

Given these views, why did Sandino not continue fighting and simply take over the entire country, after all his army was undefeated and at the height of its power? The main reason was that, despite his growing radicalism and populism, Sandino was not a true revolutionary or a political theorist. Apart from a few sketchy ideas about cooperatives, he had no blueprint for society and no desire to dismantle the structures of government. He was above all a nationalist who fought to create the conditions for reform, and as such, he rejected imported political models, including Communism. Although in the early years of his struggle he had

Communist support—one of his top advisers was a Communist, and his international solidarity movement was led by Communists—he soon quarreled with them, and the ties were severed amid bitter recriminations. The break with the Communists had repercussions that contributed to his decision to quit. It meant that once he achieved his ambition of expelling the marines, he had no political agenda to pursue to justify continuing the fight. The break also severed one of his few sources of financial support: by the beginning of 1933 he was short of ammunition and his troops were exhausted.

But both Somoza and Sacasa were convinced that Sandino had larger political ambitions and suspected that he might be using the peace to prepare again for war. That view was reinforced first in March, when Sandino's men surrendered no less than 500 rifles, and again in August, when during unrest in the capital Sandino cabled Sacasa that he could provide 600 armed men. He claimed that, through a lucky break, weapons for the extra 500 had just that moment been acquired from defeated Honduran rebels!

Tacho was horrified that Sandino could still field so many troops, but Sacasa seemed to think he could restrain Sandino, and he was soon more concerned about the loyalty of his own army. Somoza had moved quickly to assert personal control over the Guardia, and he challenged Sacasa's appointments. At the same time he apparently decided to test Sandino's will by allowing his patrols to clash with and kill some of Sandino's followers in the north.

Sandino responded with a loud campaign denouncing the Guardia as unconstitutional and demanding that it be disbanded. He also refused to disarm his remaining hundred troops on the first anniversary of the peace treaty, as had been agreed. Faced with the growing threat from Somoza, on February 19, 1934, Sacasa accepted Sandino's demands to reform the Guardia and agreed to appoint one of Sandino's supporters as presidential delegate for the north, with authority over the Guardia in that area. For Somoza and his fellow officers it was the last straw.

On the evening of February 21st, while Sandino enjoyed a pleasant dinner with Sacasa, Somoza met with his high command to discuss a plan code-named "The Death of Caesar."[15] Around midnight, as Sandino's car emerged from the presidential palace, it was stopped by National Guardsmen. He and two of his generals were seized, bundled off to the local airfield, executed by firing squad, and buried under the runway in the middle of the night. Somoza later claimed he had the support of the U.S. ambassador for his action. Recently discovered police files in Nicaragua appear to back that view, but other evidence seems to show that the ambassador was kept in the dark and tried to stop the plot.[16] Whatever the truth, many Nicaraguans simply assumed that the Yankees had conspired to assassinate their hero and had condoned the next step: the Guardia attacked Sandino's base camp in the north and massacred more than 300 men, women, and children. Over the next three years the Guardia pursued Sandino's followers, destroying their cooperatives and burning their crops.

The Seeds of Dictatorship

Sacasa knew he was next. For the following two years, as he and Somoza tussled for power, Managua was wracked by plots, counterplots, explosions, and demonstrations. As usual the Liberals and Conservatives were grappling for power, and led respectively by José Maria Moncada and Emiliano Chamorro, they conspired with the emerging strongman. To weaken Sacasa, Somoza encouraged strikes and protests while his supporters made speeches describing him favorably as a Nicaraguan Hitler who would save the country from anarchy. In one respect they were correct. Somoza gave money and weapons to a gang of fascist thugs called the "blueshirts," who beat up opponents and burned down newspapers critical of the general.

Meanwhile the presidential palace and Guardia barracks, which faced each other, were turned into enemy fortresses bristling with guns and bunkers. At one point

Sacasa's wife even persuaded the Honduran air force to bomb Somoza's headquarters. The plan, which could have tipped the whole of Central America into war, was only halted by pressure from Washington. But it was the last time such influence was exercised. The State Department revised its policy and refused to become involved in Nicaragua's internal affairs. Also, in an official announcement, the White House revoked the practice of refusing to recognize Latin American governments which came to power by force. To Somoza it seemed like a nod from Washington, a tacit encouragement to stage a coup d'etat.

In 1936 he decided to act. He sent his troops to attack the garrison of León, commanded by Sacasa's cousin, which was apart from the palace guard the last army unit loyal to the president. Sacasa was forced to admit defeat: on June 6th he resigned. For the next six months Tacho busily prepared for the elections. He bribed politicians; he summoned a Liberal Party conference, which obediently nominated him for president; he announced that the Guardia would supervise all aspects of the election, including the count; and he resigned briefly as Jefe Director of the Guardia to satisfy the constitutional requirement barring the army commander from seeking the presidency. Somoza was opposed by Dr. Leonardo Arguello, a Liberal who also had Conservative support. The effort was useless. On December 18th the results were announced: 107,201 votes for Somoza, 169 votes for Arguello. On the same day the general announced that he would resume his role as Jefe Director of the Guardia. The combination of jobs gave him immense power. It was the birth of the Somoza dictatorship, which was to last longer than any other in Latin America—until July 19, 1979.

FOUR

THE SOMOZA DYNASTY AND THE TRIUMPH OF THE SANDINISTAS

Somoza moved fast to cement his power. He persuaded his defeated adversary, Dr. Arguello, to rally Liberal support behind his government. Politicians were bribed with government posts or cash, and those who refused to stay silent were arrested or harassed. A newly formed army intelligence service spied on opponents, and newspapers were censored. The Guardia assumed control of virtually every important institution in the country: tax collection, the railways, the postal service, the national health service, the radio stations, the telephone network, immigration and emigration. Before long it even became necessary to secure a permit from the Guardia to start a new business. To complete his stranglehold the general packed a new Constituent Assembly with his supporters, rewrote the constitution, and had himself "elected" president by this body to serve until 1947.

In case anyone should get any ideas about rebelling, he fostered the rumor that he was a close personal friend of President Franklin Delano Roosevelt and that Roosevelt would intervene to protect him in the event of a revolt. The whispering campaign was helped in 1939 when he made a

The Nicaraguan National Guard, created with U.S. support, helped maintain the Somoza family dynasty.

state visit to Washington and was received at the White House with full honors. After their meeting Roosevelt commented, "Somoza's a sonofabitch but he's *our* sonofabitch."[1] The message quickly spread along the grapevine. Three other initiatives from the U.S. War Department were interpreted by Nicaraguans as evidence that Uncle Sam was determined to protect Somoza: a naval base was built at the port of Corinto; an American officer was appointed to run the Guardia's military academy; and Tacho was sent weapons worth hundreds of thousands of dollars under the Lend-Lease program. In reality the administration was probably most concerned with ensuring regional stability as the storm clouds of World War II started to gather.

The general worked hard at cultivating relations with the U.S. He renamed Managua's main street Avenida Roosevelt and proclaimed a two-day national holiday when Roosevelt was reelected in 1940. He even declared war on Japan, Germany, and Italy in December 1941. The chiefs of staff in Washington welcomed such gestures and drafted plans to incorporate the Guardia into U.S. forces in the event of an emergency. From Tacho's point of view, the declaration of war had another purpose; he used it to justify imposing a state of siege and to suspend constitutional guarantees. Those decrees allowed more repression and more corruption.

Building the Family Business

From the moment he seized power, Somoza used a variety of corrupt tactics to build his personal fortune. For example, all government employees were required to contribute 5 percent of their salaries to the Liberal Party, whose bank account Tacho used as if it were his own. In 1942, under pretext of war, he expropriated some of the country's best coffee estates from German landowners (a maneuver employed by all the region's dictators). Beef exporters had to pay him a levy of one and a half cents per pound. Private businesses, such as mining and textiles, were also induced to make "donations" to the dictator's favorite charity: himself. Much of this money was used to buy real estate. Typically Somoza would approach the owner of a property he fancied and offer half its value. If the owner were foolish enough to reject the offer, he would find himself financially and physically harassed into submission. Somoza then used government funds to build access roads to his new estates and sent government employees to work on his farms.

Within just three years he had accumulated an estimated $3 to $4 million. Over the next forty years his family would come to own or control the national airline, the national shipping line, 20 percent of the nation's agricultural land, major port installations, shopping malls, the two television stations, newspapers, and large parts of the banking system, the insurance industry, the textile industry, the construction industry, the fishing industry, and several manufacturing industries, as well as land holdings in Costa Rica, Mexico, the United States, and Canada. By the time the Somozas fled Nicaragua in 1979, the family's worth was estimated at between $500 million and $1.5 billion.[2]

Inevitably the Guardia followed Tacho's example. From the war minister down, the army became a sort of mobsters' empire, specializing in cattle rustling, gambling, smuggling, prostitution, and "protection." The Guardia became totally alienated from Nicaraguan society. Just as Somoza relied on the Guardia to stay in power, the Guardia came to rely on Somoza for immunity from prosecution and for its raison d'être. In effect the Guardia became Tacho's private bodyguard.

This situation led to growing discontent, especially among university students and the middle class. Somoza had to deal with two armed rebellions, street demonstrations, and even a split inside his own Liberal Party. Eventually, in 1947, faced with pressure from President Harry Truman's administration, he agreed not to seek reelection. Instead he nominated his puppet, Leonardo Arguello. The opposition once again legitimized the electoral game by nominating an opponent, Enoc Aguado, who was undoubtedly the more popular of the two candidates. Somoza simply released forged election results declaring Arguello the winner. To Tacho's consternation Arguello immediately showed unwelcome signs of independence. Within less than four weeks Somoza deposed him and replaced him with a more amenable stooge.

In 1949 he made a deal with the Conservative Party leaders: they agreed to put up a presidential candidate who would be allowed to lose, and in return they accepted bribes and minority participation in the government. So in 1950 Tacho resumed the presidency. These actions disturbed the White House. The Truman administration had been even more annoyed at Somoza's interference in Costa Rica's civil war in 1948, but the general ensured U.S. support with a loud propaganda campaign against communism. He also offered to send troops to Korea, and in 1954 he supported the CIA-backed overthrow of the elected Social Democrat government of Jacobo Arbenz in Guatemala.

The Dictator Is Dead—
Long Live the Dictator!

In 1956 Somoza decided to trample the constitution once again by standing for reelection. For one person at least it was too much. On September 21st, at a reception to celebrate his nomination as the Liberal Party candidate for the presidency, a nationalist poet named Rigoberto Lopez Perez drew a revolver and pumped four bullets into Tacho. Anastasio Somoza García was rushed to a U.S. military hospital in Panama, and President Dwight Eisenhower sent his best doctors to treat the man he called "a friend of the United States."[3] It was no use; on September 29, 1956, the dictator breathed his last.

But the dictatorship did not expire with him. Tacho had planned his succession too carefully for that. His elder son Luis Somoza had already been elected president of the Congress and "First Designate" for the presidency. Even before Tacho was officially pronounced dead, Luis had taken over. By February 1957 Luis had arranged to be formally "elected" president. He was aided by his younger brother Anastasio Somoza Debayle. Anastasio, Jr., nicknamed Tachito, had trained at West Point. According to a popular joke he was the only cadet from the academy ever to be given an army as a graduation present. In effect when Anastasio, Sr., died, his younger son already commanded the Guardia. In revenge for his father's assassination, Tachito rounded up hundreds of known critics of the government. Many were jailed and tortured, some were shot.

However Luis Somoza, a graduate of Louisiana State

University, decided to put a more tolerant face on the regime. When his term expired in 1963 he did not insist on succeeding himself. He nominated instead a faithful supporter, René Schick. Although the Conservative Party officially boycotted the 1963 election, Luis was able to persuade some Conservatives to provide Schick with token opposition. He lifted some censorship and even spent some money on public housing. But the Guardia continued to run rampant, and the Somozas had to face dozens of rebellions that were put down with varying degrees of brutality. Nevertheless the regime continued to retain U.S. support by following Tacho's example of catering to American interests: in 1961 Cuban exiles were allowed to use Nicaragua as the principal base for their unsuccessful CIA-backed Bay of Pigs invasion; in 1965 Nicaraguan troops joined U.S. forces in the occupation of the Dominican Republic; and in 1967 Tachito even offered to send Guardia units to fight in Vietnam. A grateful Pentagon responded with large amounts of military assistance.

In 1967, despite furious opposition from Luis, Tachito insisted on being president. Opposition parties which espoused "exotic ideologies" were banned by the constitution, which left the traditional Conservative Party, the splinter Independent Liberal Party, and the newly created Social Christian Party. These three groups united behind a single candidate, Dr. Fernando Aguero, and on January 22nd they led a demonstration of some 50,000 people through the center of Managua. The Guardia opened fire with machine guns and tanks, and perhaps as many as 600 people were killed. For several days the leaders of the march sought refuge in the luxury Gran Hotel, while the Guardia hunted down demonstrators, beating and arresting them. A few days later Tachito was formally declared to have won the election.

Three months later, in April 1967, Luis Somoza suffered a severe heart attack. President Lyndon Johnson sent his personal specialist to help, in vain. Luis died and with

Anastasio Somoza Debayle ruled Nicaragua from 1967 until his overthrow by the FSLN in 1979. Son of Anastasio Somoza Garcia, he was called the "only West Point cadet to receive an army as a graduation present."

him went the last restraining influence on Tachito. The new president, Luis's brother Anastasio, Jr., became the third Somoza in the dynasty to rule Nicaragua. Tachito had none of his brother's subtlety. He packed the cabinet, diplomatic service, state industries, and armed forces with his relatives and cronies. Corruption worsened, Liberal allies openly displayed their disenchantment, guerrilla activity increased, and the Guardia was torn by two very public murders within its own ranks.

These events appeared to threaten Somoza's power base. However he was saved by U.S. Ambassador Turner Shelton, who arranged for Tachito to be invited to a private, but well-publicized, dinner at the White House with President Richard Nixon. Shelton also organized a public meeting with United Nations Secretary-General U Thant and persuaded the American billionaire Howard Hughes to invest in Nicaragua. These moves strengthened the dictator's grip. Shelton also had a solution to the problem of Somoza's reelection in 1971. He persuaded the opposition leader Fernando Aguero to accept a deal: the Congress was dissolved, a Constituent Assembly was convened to write a new constitution, and in the meantime the country was governed by a triumvirate of two Somoza nominees and Aguero. But real power remained in Tachito's hands. Once again the leaders of the traditional parties had accepted a deal brokered by the U.S. that was beneficial to them but betrayed the aspirations of the majority of Nicaraguans.[4]

The Beginning of the End

Nevertheless the arrangement ensured relative stability until December 23, 1972, when a huge earthquake destroyed Managua. Some 10,000 people died, 50,000 were injured, 200,000 made homeless.[5] The Guardia disintegrated; troops either rushed off to search for their families or looted the stores that were not destroyed. For two days Somoza could not assemble even one company of men, and the country was on the verge of anarchy. Once again Shelton

The December 1972 earthquake in Managua left 10,000 dead, 50,000 injured, and 200,000 homeless. Somoza's corrupt management of the relief effort helped bring about his downfall.

came to the rescue, encouraging Somoza to abolish the triumvirate and to rule by decree.

Order was restored, the Guardia patrolled the streets, set up law courts, and increased its racketeering. International relief supplies were seized and sold on the black market. Bribes were demanded for rationed food supplies, for guarding damaged property, and for granting new construction permits. Somoza himself diverted foreign donations into his bank accounts. Some money did get to the National Emergency Committee, which Tachito headed. It was used to pay premium prices for land for rehousing, land Somoza and his friends had earlier bought for themselves at knockdown prices. The land was sold to the committee through Somoza's real estate agency, which took its cut. Then Somoza's construction firms were given the housing contracts. They built flimsy housing, subsequently sold at many times its cost, or luxury villas for Guardia officers. Somoza's companies were contracted to do the demolition work and to supply the building materials.

Tachito probably made $100 million out of the disaster. In Nicaragua it is widely believed that Somoza even seized emergency supplies of blood, flown in by the Red Cross, and resold them to private hospitals in the United States. True or not, soon after the earthquake Somoza and a partner founded a clinic that did indeed sell blood plasma to the U.S.[6]

This greed not only provoked ordinary people to increasingly militant demonstrations of opposition, but angered his traditional supporters among the wealthy elite, who complained that Somoza was squeezing their profits and muscling in on their traditional businesses. From that point, more and more members of the country's wealthiest families started to join the guerrillas fighting Somoza. And that year, for the first time, the Catholic Church criticized the dictatorship. Thus, 1972 marked the beginning of the end of the Somoza dynasty.

El Frente Sandinista de Liberación Nacional

The principal architect of Somoza's fall was a guerrilla group called the Sandinista National Liberation Front (FSLN; see glossary for a list of acronyms). It was founded in July 1961 by three young radicals plotting in lonely exile in Honduras. They were Carlos Fonseca, Tomas Borge, and Silvio Mayorga. They were motivated by several factors:

- They were Marxists, determined to overthrow not just Somoza but the entire economic structure in order to create a society ruled for the benefit of workers and peasants.

- They despised the traditional opposition parties for "collaborating" with the dictatorship during more than two decades of farcical elections and token democracy. They believed the opposition was interested only in establishing a "Somozism without Somoza" in which a small elite would continue to exploit the masses.
- They believed that Somoza could never be defeated by anything other than military means.
- They were fiercely nationalist and anti-American, convinced that the United States had crushed Nicaraguan independence and had helped impose and sustain the dictatorship.
- They were inspired by the example of Fidel Castro in Cuba, who in 1959 after a long guerrilla campaign had overthrown the Batista dictatorship.
- They believed that what Sandino had accomplished could be repeated. At Fonseca's insistence they named their movement after Sandino. Their ideology was a unique fusion of socialism, nationalism, and Sandinism.

At first *El Frente*, as it is commonly called in Nicaragua, simply copied Castro's example. Groups of idealistic middle-class youths marched into the mountains to confront the Guardia, hoping to inspire the peasantry to rebel simply by their example and presence. In 1963 a column of sixty was quickly decimated by the Guardia. Amid dozens of unrelated uprisings at the time, the effort went almost unnoticed. For the next four years the FSLN built a small network of peasant supporters and raided banks to finance its operations.

They were helped in these efforts by the ongoing process of concentration in land ownership brought on by a boom in cotton. Since the 1950s, thousands of peasants had been thrown off their farms. Land that had once been used to grow cereals was turned over to cotton. By 1979, throughout the country, just 1,600 people would own nearly half of all the agricultural land. On the west coast the World Bank found that "fewer than 750 farms had more than two thirds of the farm land," while 50,000 families, a quarter of the rural population, were landless and desperate.[7] The United Nations Economic Commission for Latin America estimated that 35 percent of the entire population was in "extreme poverty."[8] It was these conditions the guerrillas decided to exploit in the sixties and early seventies.

In 1967 a fresh attempt was made to establish a guerrilla front, this time in Matagalpa—part of Sandino's old stamping-ground. But once again the Guardia discovered the column and rapidly defeated it, killing Silvio Mayorga in the process. Tachito, in charge of the Guardia, ordered his men to flush out all peasant sympathizers and dispose of them. The fighting in the mountains, the repression of the peasants, and the outrage over the January massacre in Managua all served to win dozens of new recruits. But this time the Frente decided it had to build a proper support network. Although minor guerrilla raids in the mountains continued, the Sandinistas now concentrated on organizing in the universities and among urban workers.

The Alliance for Progress

The success of Castro's revolution and the failure of a U.S.-backed invasion of Cuba, known as the Bay of Pigs operation, had made the administration of President John F. Kennedy fear spreading revolution and Soviet influence throughout Latin America. The response had been twofold: military and economic. On the military front U.S. Army special forces were increased to five times their previous strength, America's rapid deployment capability was improved, and a major research program was set up to investigate counter-insurgency techniques. In addition U.S. military and police training programs for Latin American officers were expanded. By the mid-sixties 5,000 or more officers were being trained each year.

Throughout the region social unrest came to be equated with Communist subversion, and the U.S. turned a blind eye as a succession of military coups were launched in the name of stability and democracy. Among the countries where soldiers decided to take control were El Salvador, Guatemala, Honduras, and the Dominican Republic. The muted American response to these events meant that in Nicaragua the Somozas felt little pressure to control human rights abuses and political repression.

The other tactic was to encourage development projects and to promote moderate social reforms. To assist in the task, in 1961 Kennedy launched the Alliance for Progress and the Peace Corps. In 1962 he set up the Agency for International Development. The Alliance for Progress had ambitious targets: $20 billion in foreign investment throughout Latin America; modernization of the regional economies and social structures; and comprehensive land reform.

But the results were disappointing, especially in the area of land reform where the local landowners were not prepared to cooperate. Another problem was that much of the money went to boosting cash crops for export, such as cotton, instead of improving food crops for domestic consumption. The investment also increased mechanization, which cut agricultural jobs. Indeed Alliance for Progress investments made the demand for land even worse: in El Salvador the number of landless peasants rose from 12 percent of the rural population in 1961, to 41 percent in 1975. On the whole the spending was not directed to the neediest. Roads, airports, and ports were developed for the benefit of those who already had the resources to pay for transportation—the wealthy and the middle-class. Moreover much of the aid was in the form of loans earmarked for the purchase of American-made goods, thus providing little incentive to local manufacturing.[9]

The Central American Common Market

In reality the Nicaraguan economy benefited more from the creation of a Central American Common Market in 1960 than from the Alliance for Progress. Nevertheless the two developments working in tandem helped create some local manufacturing industries, mainly those related to the primary cash crops. For example, cooking-oil factories processed cotton seeds, a by-product of the cotton harvest. The oil was sold to other Central American countries and to the local market. Between 1960 and 1967 Nicaragua's economy grew at an astonishing annual rate of 10.7 percent, and the number of factory workers grew proportionately.[10]

Factory workers became a relatively privileged group. They had better wages and access to some medical care and education. But Central America is a limited market, and the manufacturing expansion soon saturated the demand. By the end of the 1960s the boom started to fizzle. The disenchanted workers became an ideal recruiting ground for the Sandinistas, and FSLN influence began to be felt in a series of strikes and demonstrations.

Despite the exponential growth of the opposition, in 1974 Tachito blithely published a new constitution, called fresh presidential elections, selected a token opposition candidate, and declared himself the winner. The elections were openly denounced by the Church and by 27 Conservative and other opposition leaders who were promptly jailed. In November of that year, for the first time, business leaders joined the traditional opposition parties in forming an anti-Somoza alliance, the Democratic Liberation Union (UDEL). But the first item on the UDEL list of demands had to do with ending the corruption and "unfair competition" from Somoza's empire that was making it difficult for small entrepreneurs to do business. In reality UDEL was a repetition of the tactic used continuously by Nicaragua's elite since the nineteenth century—a wealthy group united in an effort to defend its narrow economic interests.[11]

The Sandinista response to the elections was more spectacular: on the night of December 27, 1974, an FSLN commando team seized a dozen of Somoza's closest supporters at a Christmas party in honor of Ambassador Shelton. After prolonged negotiations Tachito was forced to accede to their demands; he released fourteen Sandinista prisoners from jail and allowed them to fly with the commando team to Cuba. He also paid a $2 million ransom and published and broadcast a lengthy political communique that denounced his regime and U.S. policy, demanded higher wages, and called on the people to rebel. For the first time the Sandinistas gained a national reputation and a groundswell of sympathy.

The Repression Grows

Tachito's response to this public humiliation was to seek bloody revenge: he declared a state of siege and the Guardia was given free rein. Over the next few months they indiscriminately jailed, tortured, raped, and executed hundreds, perhaps thousands, of peasants in Matagalpa. Houses and crops were even napalmed and bombed from the air. These excesses were reported by Catholic priests[12] and became the target of an inquiry by the U.S. Congress and by the Amnesty International human rights group. Somoza found himself increasingly vilified in the world press, and in 1976 this resulted in his being denied a major loan by the Inter-American Development Bank.

Yet his campaign of terror had some success. In 1976 Carlos Fonseca was ambushed and killed, and Tomas Borge was jailed. Meanwhile the pressure caused the FSLN to split into three factions. It was a division over tactics not goals. One faction argued for a slow accumulation of forces by educating and recruiting workers and peasants for a long war. Another faction argued for concentrating on trade unions and urban organizations to create the conditions for an insurrection in the capital. The third faction (Terceristas) argued for building a broad temporary alliance with all forces opposed to Somoza and using daring guerrilla operations to stir people to rebel immediately.

The combination of this split and the repression led

Somoza to believe that he had crushed all opposition. Throughout 1977 he came under mounting pressure from the administration of President Jimmy Carter, the International Commission of Jurists, the Church, and the private businessmen's organization COSEP. Finally in September he ended the state of siege and lifted censorship. In October the Terceristas responded by attacking Guardia barracks in three towns and by persuading twelve of the most prominent men in the country to release a letter stating their belief that there could be no solution to the Nicaraguan crisis without the participation of the FSLN.

The "Group of Twelve" (*los Doce*) included priests, lawyers, businessmen, academics, and other professionals. In one blow the letter legitimized the guerrilla effort to overthrow Somoza.[13] Suddenly UDEL and the conservative opposition started to demand a "national dialogue"; it was clear that they feared the possibility of a left-wing guerrilla takeover. They hoped to persuade Somoza to leave the country peacefully, but they had no plans to dismantle the Guardia or any clear plan of social change.

The Spark—Assassination

The letter of Los Doce had been published in the opposition newspaper *La Prensa,* which also ran a concerted campaign of attacks on Somoza. *La Prensa* was edited by Pedro Joaquin Chamorro. Chamorro had led an early guerrilla attack against the first Somoza, he had created UDEL, and he was one of the few Conservative leaders who consistently and actively campaigned against the dictatorship. For 20 years he had been in and out of the Somozas' jails. As a result he was extremely popular. On January 10, 1978, as he drove through the center of Managua, Chamorro was cut down in a hail of machine-gun fire. It has never been established who exactly ordered the assassination, but the people blamed Somoza. Next day they rioted. They set fire to fifteen Somoza businesses, starting with the "House of Dracula"—the blood plasma export clinic. More than 100,000 attended the funeral procession.

The businessmen tried to seize the initiative from the Sandinistas by declaring a "civil stoppage." For two weeks there was a general strike, punctuated by bloody clashes with the Guardia. In the beginning of February, the Sandinistas attacked two more Guardia barracks. Finally on February 20th the Indian inhabitants of Monimbo, in the town of Masaya, launched a full-blown insurrection. The Sandinistas sent guerrillas to organize the fighting. For a week they battled the Guardia. Finally, backed by tanks, artillery, and air strikes, the Guardia suppressed the revolt. Afterward youths were picked up and executed on the streets or simply disappeared. Some escaped with hands or tongues lopped off. But most Nicaraguans did not see it as a defeat. The example of a popular rebellion had been established and dozens more joined the FSLN.[14]

The Sandinistas kept the pressure up with a wave of strikes and demonstrations, and they continued to organize and recruit in the slums and factories. As tension escalated, the traditional parties tried to direct the course of events. In March a Managua millionaire, Alfonso Robelo, created a new party called the Nicaraguan Democratic Movement (MDN) which called for Somoza's ouster, for democratic reforms, and for the involvement of the FSLN in a new government. In May, with strong encouragement from the U.S. embassy, the MDN and UDEL created a new opposition coalition which included the FSLN sympathizers from Los Doce. It was called the Broad Opposition Front (FAO). At the same time the Carter White House was pressing Somoza to respect human rights and to allow free elections.

Somoza's reaction was typical. In June 1978 he created an elite new battalion within the Guardia known by its Spanish initials as the EEBI, standing for Basic Infantry Training School. The EEBI was commanded by Tachito's son

Anastasio Somoza Portacarrero. Known by his nickname "El Chiguin," Anastasio 3rd was even more brutal than his father. This, for example, was the call-and-response for a routine EEBI training drill: "Who are we? We are tigers. What do tigers eat? Blood. Whose blood? The blood of the people."[15] The EEBI even used a mentally retarded 12-year-old boy to torture their prisoners by digging their eyes out with a spoon.[16] Not surprisingly, even regular Guardia troops were terrified of the EEBI.

One Thousand Hostages

On August 22nd the Sandinistas took advantage of that fear in a daring raid: twenty-five guerrillas, commanded by Eden Pastora and disguised as EEBI troops, drove up to the National Palace where the Congress was in session. They shouted "The boss is coming," and the terrified palace guards surrendered their weapons. Within minutes the Sandinistas controlled the whole building and captured two of Somoza's relatives, fifty congressmen and more than a thousand other hostages. Somoza was forced to give in to their demands: he released fifty-eight Sandinista prisoners, paid a $500,000 ransom, and published and broadcast extensive Sandinista political communiqués. As they drove to the airport with their hostages, thousands of cheering people lined the roads shouting "Death to Somoza." From Managua the guerrillas flew to Panama and Venezuela, and those two countries began to supply the FSLN with weapons, many of them donated by Cuba.[17] The roundabout supply route from Havana was used to avoid raising suspicions in the U.S.

The next day the Broad Opposition Front (FAO) made another attempt to seize the initiative by calling another, indefinite, general strike. On September 9th the FSLN struck back with simultaneous attacks on Guardia barracks in five cities and a call for an insurrection, which was answered in at least ten towns. The fighting lasted for nearly

Sandinista guerrillas during the insurrection that overthrew Somoza

two weeks, cities were bombed from the air, and several thousand people died before the uprising was crushed. But again the Sandinistas emerged strengthened as thousands of new recruits flocked to their training camps in Costa Rica and the Nicaraguan mountains.

In December the three FSLN factions reunited. By March they had created a nine-member Dirección Nacional (DN) or National Directorate, made up of three leaders from each faction. Seven of the nine were under forty years of age. Ever since 1979 there have been reports of bitter arguments between the members of the DN. According to these accounts the leader of the Prolonged Popular War faction, Tomas Borge, was seen as a hard-line Marxist-Leninist who constantly tried to push the FSLN to be more left-wing and repressive. The Tercerista faction, led by Humberto Ortega and his brother Daniel, was seen as more moderate and prepared to make alliances with non-Marxists. Whatever the private reality, no public proof of such divisions has ever been allowed to surface. In public the DN has always maintained its unity. But in 1979 the Tercerista faction clearly dominated FSLN tactics, and many middle-class Nicaraguans hoped that its "moderation" could be used to steer the FSLN toward some sort of Western European–style social democracy.

The CIA, however, was convinced that the Sandinistas were Communists. The Carter administration suddenly woke to the possibility of a Marxist guerrilla victory in Central America and persuaded Somoza to accept a team from the Organization of American States (OAS) to negotiate with the FAO. When the FAO proposed a new government that would include representatives of Somoza's Liberal Party, the representatives of Los Doce withdrew. For them no compromise was possible. Somoza pretended to consider the FAO proposal. Yet the Carter administration could not decide whether or not to force Somoza's immediate resignation as a means of helping the traditional opposition take power. The negotiations sputtered on for four months.

The Sandinistas used the time to stockpile weapons, to seek international assistance, to organize their leadership, and to train their new recruits, some of whom were sent to Cuba for artillery practice. Somoza used the time to liquidate his assets and send millions of dollars abroad and to increase the size of the Guardia. On January 19th, believing himself once again in control, Somoza rejected the OAS mediators' final proposal. On February 8th the White House responded by cutting all military and economic aid to the dictator, but he continued to receive arms from Israel. The traditional opposition were now faced with an uncomfortable choice: to make peace with Somoza or to throw in their lot with the FSLN. The FAO dithered in confusion.

The Final Insurrection

On May 29th 300 Sandinista guerrillas commanded by Eden Pastora invaded Nicaragua from Costa Rica. They succeeded in their task of pinning down Somoza's elite troops. The Sandinistas called for a general insurrection, announcing that "the hour of the overthrow of the infamous dictatorship has come." They immediately seized the vital city of León, and a general strike quickly paralyzed the country. The Sandinista tactic was to strike in so many different areas at once that the Guardia would have to disperse and would become vulnerable and ineffective. It worked. Civilians in virtually every town and village built barricades, made homemade bombs, and attacked Guardia posts. One by one towns began to fall to the guerrillas.

On June 16th a five-member revolutionary Junta (a government in exile) was announced in Costa Rica—Violeta (widow of Pedro Joaquin) Chamorro, Alfonso Robelo, and three Sandinistas. But the White House was still looking for other alternatives. Then Somoza's brutal Guardia claimed an American life. On June 21st an ABC TV news team was filming the fighting in Managua's slums. An American correspondent, Bill Stewart, was stopped by a Guardia officer, made to lie on the ground, and then shot in cold blood. The episode was caught on film and beamed into millions of American homes. In the United States public opinion clamored for an end to U.S. support for the dictator.

But the White House was still trying to prevent an outright Sandinista victory and on June 23rd called for an OAS peacekeeping force to be sent to Nicaragua. The OAS rejected the proposal. At the beginning of July the U.S. demanded an expanded Junta to dilute the Marxist influence. The Sandinistas agreed, but Violeta Chamorro refused. On July 12th the Junta wrote to the OAS, promising to call Nicaraguans to "the first free elections they will have in this century"[18] and to incorporate any Guardias who surrendered into the new national army. Two days later the Junta announced an eighteen-member cabinet that included only one Sandinista leader, Tomas Borge.

These moves allayed some fears in Washington and in the FAO, but still American diplomats scrambled to prevent a Sandinista victory. They pieced together a complicated plan: Somoza would resign and a new president would take over briefly who would appoint a new head of the Guardia to negotiate a ceasefire and an amalgamation of the Sandinista and Guardia forces. Only then would power be handed over to the Junta. On July 17th Somoza duly resigned, and a virtual unknown named Francisco Urcuyo Malianos was sworn in. But Urcuyo refused to hand over power; instead he ordered the Guardia to fight on. The Sandinistas were happy to see the fight through to the bitter end. On July 18th Somoza and a hundred of his closest aides and relatives fled. The Guardia thus lost its sole raison d'être. As the news spread, many Guardias threw away their guns and uniforms and tried to escape by boat, plane, and by road to Honduras. On July 18th the Junta flew into León, and that same day columns from León and from Masaya started advancing toward Managua. On the 19th they started to pour into the capital, and a Guardia officer formally surrendered. The day was simply christened El Triunfo (the Triumph).

FIVE

THE HONEYMOON

On July 20th the new Junta drove into Managua, to be greeted in the main plaza by an ecstatic crowd of tens of thousands of people. Many Nicaraguans recall those first days and months with nostalgia. There was a heady feeling in the air. "Overthrowing Somoza had seemed impossible, so after that building a utopia would be easy, all it would take was enthusiasm," one young Nicaraguan said of the mood at the time.[1] Government bureaucrats, whether Socialists or Conservatives, worked together for long hours at little pay to repair the damage of the war. Teams of unpaid volunteers dedicated hundreds of thousands of hours building roads and parks, vaccinating children, and teaching people to read. But the problems facing the new government were extraordinary.

The Inheritance

To start with, the country was bankrupt. Somoza had raided the treasury before he fled, leaving just $3.5 million in cash reserves, enough to pay the national import bill for only two days.[2] The dictatorship had racked up a $1.6-billion foreign debt; the repayments scheduled for 1979 alone amounted to more than Nicaragua's total export earnings that year.[3] Nearly two thirds of the country's businessmen had fled, taking with them at least $500 million.[4]

Both industry and agriculture had been decimated by the war. When the dictator sent his planes to bomb the Managua neighborhoods where the fighting was most intense, he also gave his pilots orders to destroy factories belonging to his business competitors. War damage was estimated at $480 million.[5] Fleeing Guardias had stolen most of the national fishing fleet. In the countryside the fighting had disrupted harvesting and planting. In 1980 exports of cotton—the second-largest foreign-exchange earner—dropped more than 80 percent, beef was down 30 percent, sugar more than 20 percent.[6]

There was no means of imposing law and order. There was no parliament, no functioning government bureaucracy. There were no police. That role had been performed, in theory, by the Guardia Nacional which had ceased to exist. There was not a single judge left in the country, nor one trained prison guard who could be trusted with the approximately 6,330 Guardias who had been captured. There was of course no army. Even the Sandinistas had no formal way of imposing authority on their own ranks: of the thousands of ragtag guerrillas who swept into Managua, only about 500 were inducted members of the Sandinista Front. For weeks after the Triumph the nights in Managua were punctured by prolonged gun battles. Marauding Guardias who slipped out of their hiding places, thieves, ultra-left guerrillas, and over-enthusiastic Sandinista volunteer militias shot at each other or at their shadows.

The social problems to be faced were also enormous. Estimates of the number killed in the fighting range between 30,000 and 50,000, and 150,000 were wounded. Yet hundreds of doctors had left the country, and there were fewer than 5,000 hospital beds in the whole of Nicaragua.

About 40,000 children had been orphaned; 500,000 people were homeless, and more than a third were unemployed. Somoza's inheritance to most Nicaraguans was a life expectancy of just 53 years. Of every 1,000 children born, approximately 120 died in their first year. The biggest child-killer was diarrhea caused by lack of sanitation; 60 percent of the urban population and 90 percent of the rural population had no access to clean drinking water. More than half the population could not read or write, earned less than $300 per year, and suffered from malnutrition.[7]

The capital itself was a symbol of the desperate poverty and neglect caused by forty years of dictatorship. What had once been 600 bustling blocks of downtown Managua was a pile of rubble and a few twisted ruins almost hidden by a jungle of 12-foot grass and weeds. Just three buildings remained intact after the 1972 earthquake: the National Palace, the Banco de America skyscraper, and the Hotel Intercontinental. Anastasio Somoza Debayle had refused to move the capital to a less earthquake-prone part of the country, probably because he had invested so much money in real estate around the outskirts of the city. For the same reason he never bothered to clear and rebuild the city center, despite promises to do so.

As a result modern-day Managua is a city without a heart, a series of low-level suburban villages and slum shantytowns connected by large tracts of dusty open space, strung out for miles around what looks like a minefield.

Mutual Suspicions

But the real minefield after El Triunfo was a political one. Right from the start, all of the actors on the political stage deeply distrusted each other. The Sandinistas despised the traditional opposition parties for having "collaborated" so long with the dictatorship. They traced an unbroken line of betrayal right back to Espino Negro and William Walker. To the Sandinistas the anti-Somoza businessmen of 1979 were modern-day *vendepatrias;* people who always sold out to the United States, and they did not believe the leopard could change its spots. Many members of the middle-class had been born or educated in the U.S., some even spoke better English than Spanish and in their outlook, the FSLN thought, they were more in tune with "Yankee" politics than the Nicaraguan reality. They were also convinced that the United States would attempt to destabilize the new government, as the CIA had tried to do in Cuba in 1961 and as it had succeeded in doing in Guatemala in 1954 and in Chile in 1973. The Sandinista hymn, written that year, contained a blunt summary of their view: "We fight against the Yankee, enemy of humanity."

But the feelings were mutual. The Carter administration had desperately tried to prevent a Sandinista-dominated government from coming to power. At the end of June the Pentagon had even reviewed its contingency plans for an invasion force and had placed the 82nd Airborne Division on alert, and in July, 130 members of Congress had written to Carter asking him to resume arms sales to Somoza. The majority view in Washington was that the Sandinistas would soon impose a Marxist dictatorship.

The pattern was repeated among domestic politicians. "Uneducated terrorists," Mario Rappaccioli, a Conservative leader called them.[8] He reflected the view of many middle-class politicians that only they were capable of ruling the country. Even before Somoza fell, Alfonso Robelo, supposedly the most left-wing and pro-Sandinista of all the businessmen, was attacking them: in March 1979 he warned that "the country will be in danger of falling under Communist rule";[9] in April he said the Sandinistas would install a "totalitarian regime."[10]

Other "moderates" felt the same way: the archbishop of Managua, Miguel Obando y Bravo; the head of the Nicaraguan Red Cross, Ismael Reyes; and the head of the Human Rights Commission, José Esteban Gonzalez, flew to Venezuela with a group of businessmen just two days before the

Triumph in an effort to prevent a Sandinista political victory. They hoped to persuade Venezuelan President Herrera Campins to force the Sandinistas to accept a bigger Junta in which the FSLN members would be in a minority. To the Sandinistas such actions were tantamount to treason.

The Role of the Revolution

The animosity was, of course, motivated by profound political differences. Although both sides agreed on the urgency of improving living conditions for the poorest Nicaraguans, they differed on how it should be done. The leaders of the traditional parties thought a few government health and education programs would do the trick. They saw no need for wholesale changes to the system. While they accepted a state role in wage and labor legislation to prevent the worst injustices of the past, they argued that economic recovery could best be guaranteed by free enterprise. The increased wealth of private businessmen and landowners, they said, would trickle down to workers through taxation. Theirs was a gradual, reformist approach that would allow the upper- and middle-classes to retain economic and political power.

But the Sandinistas wanted a much faster solution. As Marxists they wanted to create a socialist society in which workers and peasants would hold political power and control the economy. They contemptuously referred to their opponents on the Right as Burgeses, or bourgeoisie, meaning a reactionary middle-class group of capitalists that would try to prevent the proletariat from seizing control (although at least some of their opponents were working-class members of non-Marxist trade unions, and some of their own top leaders were members of Nicaragua's richest families). Since most peasants and slum-dwellers were illiterate and had no experience of political or economic power, they would clearly need leaders to direct the transformation of society. The FSLN saw itself as that leadership or "vanguard."

The prospect of Sandinista domination and of a socialist society worried the middle- and upper-class leaders. But at first sight they had little to fear. Although Sandinistas outnumbered their opponents by three to two on the Junta, which was the supreme executive authority, only three of the 18 members of the cabinet were Sandinistas. Wealthy businessmen and landowners held the vital Ministries of Planning, Industry, Finance, and Agriculture. A deserter from Somoza's Guardia, Colonel Bernardino Larios, was Minister of Defense. A Conservative banker, Arturo Cruz, was president of the Central Bank, and members of Alfonso Robelo's MDN held some of the most crucial posts throughout the fledgling government bureaucracy. While still in exile in Costa Rica, the Junta had announced a plan of government that committed the FSLN to political pluralism, to freedom of speech and religion, and to an unaligned foreign policy. After the Triumph a newly adopted Code of Rights and an interim constitution, called the Fundamental Law of the state, appeared to assure democracy and respect for individual rights.

Moreover the Sandinistas had never been rigidly dogmatic about the shape of the new society: in two volumes of collected writings the Sandinistas' foremost theoretician, Carlos Fonseca, did not once refer to a government program in anything but the wooliest of terms: "land for the peasants, no more exploitation or misery, emancipation of women" ran one wish list.[11] Fonseca insisted that Sandinista theory should relate to the practical experiences of the guerrilla movement, and he boasted of the "extremely modest theoretical tradition" of the FSLN.[12] Indeed, for a revolutionary movement the FSLN had been remarkably pragmatic in establishing broad class alliances during the fight against Somoza. Those alliances had been crucial in motivating mass support for the final insurrection and in ensuring the success of crippling strikes. The Sandinistas had also worked hard at wooing non-Socialist governments such as those in Venezuela, Mexico, and West Germany. Those governments, and others in Latin America and Western

Europe, were valuable sources of development aid. The Sandinistas immediately made it clear that, despite their reservations, they were determined to preserve national unity and their new international friendships.

Even though they commanded a majority on the Junta, the Sandinistas were thus careful to avoid actions that might seem too radical. The Junta immediately decreed nationalization of all Somoza's property and of the banks and foreign trade, but many Burgeses sympathized with these moves as essential to give the government the power it needed to jump-start the economy. In October the insurance and mining industries were also nationalized, but at the same time the FSLN promised to respect private property. The death penalty was immediately abolished, and there were no widespread acts of revenge against Somocistas. In fact the first opponents of the Sandinistas to be arrested were not from the bourgeoisie, but from the Popular Action Movement (MAP), one of four ultra-left parties that attacked the Sandinistas for not being sufficiently revolutionary. The Trotskyist MAP refused to disarm its militias after the revolution. It urged workers to seize factories, and to strike for extravagant wage claims, and it preached that a second revolution would be necessary to expel the FSLN.[13] In August and again in January 1980 MAP leaders were arrested and their newspaper closed. In May, Communist Party leaders were also arrested for leading a wave of damaging strikes. Apart from these actions political parties were totally free to organize, recruit, and campaign, and the opposition press was not censored.

Consolidating Sandinista Power

In theory this left both sides free to compete for power in the political vacuum created by the disintegration of the dictatorship. But in reality the Sandinistas were the only ones with guns, and they commanded immense popularity and moral authority which their middle-class allies did not.

There was no question that throughout the country it was the FSLN that was generally credited with having engineered Somoza's fall. "If they had organized an election in the first year they would have won an overwhelming majority of the votes," the leader of the Social Christian Party, Agustin Jarquin, admitted later.[14] The Sandinistas argued that amid the devastation of the war, and with a majority of the population unable to read or write, it did not make sense to hold immediate elections. At first the argument was widely accepted abroad and by some of the domestic opposition. But in any case the Sandinistas had no taste for elections. "The people voted on July 19th, they voted with blood and bullets, and they will defend their victory in the same way," Tomas Borge was fond of saying. Although they were prepared to accept the Burgeses as junior partners in government, the Sandinistas believed the military victory had been a vote of confidence in the FSLN.

The Sandinistas moved fast to capitalize on the sudden and explosive growth in their support. The nine-man National Directorate of the FSLN became almost a second cabinet, wielding virtual executive authority in the confusion of the last days of fighting and in the immediate aftermath of victory. The Junta was assigned the task of rebuilding the economy, but the Sandinistas undertook to build an army and mobilize mass support for the revolution. In the first months this created a sort of balance of power between Right and Left: the bourgeoisie controlled most of the economy and government bureaucracy, and the Sandinistas controlled the army, police, and the biggest political and trade union organizations.

During the insurrection, encouraged by the FSLN, many neighborhoods had founded Civil Defense Committees, which built barricades, posted sentries, manufactured homemade bombs, and effectively became local governments. After the Triumph the FSLN encouraged every city block to retain these committees. They were renamed Sandi-

Sandinista volunteers organized by local block committees guard their neighborhood against crime and "counterrevolutionary activity."

nista Defense Committees (CDSs) and given a regional and national structure. They were told they would be the "eyes, ears, and voice" of the revolution. By the end of 1979 there were 10,000 to 15,000 CDS committees. They organized voluntary work such as vaccination campaigns and nighttime Revolutionary Vigilance patrols of neighborhoods to prevent crime and to investigate suspicious activity. Over the months their responsibilities grew to include important activities such as distribution of rationed food. Though membership in the CDS was voluntary, those who refused in the early months were often accused of being "counterrevolutionaries."

The Sandinistas also founded a trade union, a peasants' organization, a women's movement, and a youth group. For months their ablest leaders raced around the country working fifteen, sometimes twenty hours a day. They gave recruiting speeches in an endless procession of dusty village squares. In some cases people were undoubtedly pressured to sign up, but by the end of 1979 hundreds of thousands of Nicaraguans had enthusiastically volunteered to join one or another of the Sandinista "mass organizations."

During this time the traditional parties were, by comparison, virtually immobile, despite the fact that they faced no repression. The MDN, the Conservatives, the Social Christians, and the Independent Liberals all held a series of meetings around the country, but attendance was sparse and they made no concerted recruiting drive. The traditional parties were divided. They had no coherent policy or any idea of how to effectively confront the Sandinistas' consolidation of power. For example, few complained on July 28th when the Sandinistas bypassed the defense minister and announced that four of their top leaders would be responsible for creation of a new army. Again there was barely a murmur on August 18th when Humberto Ortega was named commander-in-chief of what was to be called the Sandinista Popular Army (EPS).

One of the defenses that the traditional parties thought they would have against Sandinista dominance was the Council of State. In June the Sandinistas had agreed that a 33-member council would be appointed after the Triumph with the power to veto the Junta's decisions. The original composition of the council consigned the Sandinistas to a minority. Yet after the Triumph it was Alfonso Robelo, a member of the bourgeoisie, who announced that the Council of State would not be convened until May 4, 1980. Not one non-Sandinista member of the government complained publicly. The opposition parties and some businessmen spoke out, but they did not organize any demonstrations or make any serious effort to reverse the decision.

Indeed the most effective opposition to the Sandinistas came not from any political party but from the private businessmen's group known by its Spanish acronym COSEP. But COSEP was so antagonistic toward the FSLN that there never appeared to be any serious attempt to cooperate with the government. Its first complaints about the revolution were made within just eleven days of the Triumph. In that brief period there is no doubt that farms and factories had been seized from people who had not been supporters of Somoza, and some people, perhaps hundreds, were unfairly arrested. But there is no evidence that those activities were conducted under orders from the National Directorate. The FSLN saw the COSEP action as an early attempt to undermine its authority.

At the same time the refusal by some large landowners and businessmen to reinvest in their companies and farms, and the efforts by others to decapitalize their businesses and secretly send funds abroad, was interpreted by the Sandinistas as deliberate economic sabotage. In many cases it was merely the product of uncertainty over the future of the private sector, especially since the Statute on the Rights of Nicaraguans released in August had stated "Property, whether individual or collective, fulfills a social function.

Therefore it may be subject to restrictions with respect to ownership, benefit, use, and disposition."[15] Reprisals against recalcitrant owners, in the form of confiscations by the state, merely led to greater insecurity. The mutual suspicion slowly evolved into open hostility.

Concepts of Democracy

Another early problem was the evidence that the FSLN did not have the same concept of a new democratic society as did the traditional parties. The Burgeses undoubtedly looked to the United States for their model of democracy. But as far as the Sandinistas were concerned, the American style of government had led to more than a hundred years of interference in Nicaraguan affairs and to the Somoza dictatorship. The only country in the region which appeared to share their concern for the working class was Cuba, and it was there that they looked for an example.

The Sandinistas believed they were creating a democracy by building a state controlled by the workers and peasants who represented an overwhelming majority of the population. Therefore they saw nothing wrong with the "vanguard" of the workers and peasants using state resources to further its objectives. So the FSLN took over the two TV stations and called them the Sandinista TV System. They seized Somoza's newspaper and turned it into a Sandinista newspaper. They confiscated the buildings used by pro-Somoza trade unions and gave them to the Sandinista union. They turned Somoza's largest mansion into the FSLN headquarters.

Most important of all, the police and army were called the "Sandinista Police" and the "Sandinista Popular Army." The opposition said this would be acceptable if the term "Sandinista" could be used by anyone who had opposed Somoza, as a sort of generic synonym for patriotism. Indeed a group of Conservative dissidents founded a new party, which they tried to call the Sandinista Social Democratic Party. But, at FSLN insistence, the Junta restricted use of the name Sandinista to FSLN organizations. The Burgeses immediately complained that this created confusion between the party and the state, and they argued it was evidence that the Sandinistas were totalitarian and would eventually impose a one-party state. The Sandinistas were unimpressed by the argument. They had seen how military men throughout Latin America had overthrown elected left-wing governments, often with CIA backing, particularly in Guatemala in 1954 and Chile in 1973. They believed control of the armed forces reflected the popular will and therefore was a defense of democracy.

COSEP's suspicions about the FSLN were strengthened in late September when a three-day meeting of top Sandinistas produced a document which described the relationship with the non-Marxists as an "alliance of convenience." The document also admitted that the FSLN did not like the June Plan of Government, which had promised political and economic pluralism. It also spoke of an "intermediate period," without spelling out what was to come.[16]

The Early Achievements

Nevertheless Sergio Ramirez, a Sandinista member of the Junta who is now vice president, insisted in 1980 that "the revolution be judged by its real social achievements . . . not by the ideological labels which some people try to pin on it."[17] Those achievements were indeed substantial. To deal with the problem of unemployment a number of labor-intensive and relatively cheap building works were started, including new markets, roads, sewerage and clean water systems, urban and rural electrification, parks, and recreation centers.

A massive vaccination program succeeded in wiping out polio and in sharply reducing other diseases. Buildings seized from Somoza were converted into old peoples' homes, orphanages, and day-care centers. Rents were halved and work started on building low-cost housing. An agrarian reform was initiated with the aim of providing plots for landless peasants, and generous bank credits were made available to help poor farmers buy seed, fertilizer, and farm implements. Paramedics were trained and sent into the countryside, rural health clinics were built, and by the end of 1979 the number of people covered by health care had increased from 30 to 70 percent of the population. By 1982 infant mortality had dropped more than 23 percent.

Above all an ambitious Literacy Crusade was launched in March 1980. About 100,000 volunteers were sent into the remotest corners of the country, and in five months they cut the illiteracy rate from more than 50 percent to less than 13 percent. The crusade was succeeded by a program of continuing adult education. Within three years more than 240,000 people had enrolled. Between 1978 and 1982 education spending more than trebled.[18] Yet even the social programs led to heated protests from COSEP, which complained, for example, that the textbooks in the Literacy Crusade were being used for "political indoctrination."

On November 14th COSEP wrote to the Junta and the National Directorate (DN) complaining bitterly that the seeds of one-party dictatorship were being sown, that property was being seized for no reason, and that they had no access to money for investment. The Sandinistas responded on November 22nd by suspending the decree authorizing property confiscations from Somocistas. They unfroze dozens of bank accounts and publicly discouraged their supporters from invading private farms and factories. The alliance with the private sector won a new lease on life.

In December there was a cabinet reshuffle. Henry Ruiz, the only member of the FSLN National Directorate to have any close links to the Soviet Union, was made minister of planning, and he quickly assembled a team of economic

In 1980, 100,000 volunteers were sent throughout Nicaragua to teach reading and writing—with impressive results.

advisers from Bulgaria. Another member of the DN, Jaime Wheelock, was made minister of agriculture. Luis Carrion, also of the DN, was made deputy defense minister to Humberto Ortega. With Borge at the Interior Ministry and Daniel Ortega in the role as coordinator of the Junta, six out of the nine DN members were now in the cabinet, and between them controlled the most crucial sectors of government. The opposition was even more fearful than before, but the uneasy alliance with the FSLN was to hold for another few months.

SIX

THE DIVORCE

The honeymoon with the United States was much briefer and less fruitful than with the domestic opposition. From the moment Somoza fled, the Sandinistas had anticipated U.S. intervention, and Washington had anticipated a Communist dictatorship. Actions by both sides made their fears seem like self-fulfilling prophecies.

Foreign Relations

The first American concern was over Cuban influence. The U.S. ambassador, Lawrence Pezzullo, arrived in Managua on July 28th with a transport plane loaded with food and medicine, but by then sixty Cuban doctors had already arrived, and a Sandinista delegation, led by Robelo and Humberto Ortega, had flown to Havana for the annual celebration of the Cuban revolution, where they were treated like visiting royalty.

Pezzullo hoped to steer the Sandinista leaders toward more "moderate" policies with economic aid and good relations.[1] He held regular meetings with members of the DN, and over the next year he managed to wring about $60 million from Washington in food, loans, and grants which arrived in small dribs and drabs. In August two U.S. officials recommended an aid package totalling $75 million, with the proviso that 60 percent be given to private businesses and most of the rest to non-governmental voluntary organizations.

The Sandinistas saw this as a blatant attempt to shape their economic policy, but desperate for cash, they went along with the idea. However the proposal was not presented to Congress until November, when the assistant secretary of state, Viron Vaky, told the House Foreign Affairs Committee that the aid was destined to help strengthen the "moderates" in their tug of war with the FSLN.[2] Despite Vaky's explanation the opposition in Congress was ferocious. At one point the House of Representatives went into secret session, for only the second time in its history, to hear testimony from the CIA that Nicaragua was already communist. The evidence was not convincing and eventually the aid was approved, but not until the fall of 1980 and even then only $60 million ever reached Managua.

By the time Congress made up its mind, Nicaragua had been promised $500 million in loans from international development banks and about $700 million in grants, loans, and aid-in-kind from governments as disparate as the Netherlands, Spain, Sweden, West and East Germany, the Soviet Union, Czechoslovakia, Rumania, Cuba, Mexico, Venezuela, Panama, Brazil, and Taiwan.[3] Thousands of volunteers and government-sponsored technicians poured in from dozens of countries. The largest contingent came from Cuba, which sent more than 2,000 teachers, doctors, engineers, military instructors, security advisers, and communications experts. Cuba also offered thousands of places to Nicaraguan high school and university students. Pezzullo frequently complained that while his hands were tied by red tape and indecision in Washington the Cubans could send help at the drop of a hat.[4]

The friendship with Cuba aside, other aspects of Sandinista foreign policy alarmed the White House. In September 1979 Daniel Ortega made a speech at a meeting of the Nonaligned Movement, bitterly attacking the history of U.S. interference in Nicaragua. He praised the revolutions in Grenada and Iran, expressed support for the PLO and the Vietnamese government, demanded U.S. withdrawal from the Guantanamo base in Cuba and the Panama Canal and called for Puerto Rican independence. He repeated much of this at the United Nations, where Nicaragua subsequently abstained on two votes to condemn the Soviet invasion of Afghanistan. Delegations from the PLO and Latin American guerrilla groups were among the first foreign visitors to Managua. Embassies were opened in Libya and the Soviet bloc. Yet despite all this, Nicaragua was far from being a Soviet proxy. In fact for a long time Moscow had opposed Sandinista efforts to topple Somoza as military "adventurism."[5] Of the DN members only Ruiz had visited Moscow before the Triumph. In Managua the Communist "hammer and sickle" was rarely seen and the word *Communist* was never used by the Sandinistas to describe their own philosophy. Indeed the Kremlin's formal ally in Nicaragua continues to be a Communist party called the Nicaraguan Socialist Party.

Building an Army

Beyond the revolutionary rhetoric there were indications of Sandinista pragmatism in international relations. For example, the first country they turned to for help in building their armed forces was the United States. In September Daniel Ortega visited President Carter to press a request for military hardware, and in November Joaquin Cuadra, chief of staff of the armed forces, toured several U.S. military bases. Pezzullo backed the request, hoping military cooperation might help reduce hostility. But there were too many obstacles. The White House suspected that weapons might be

Daniel Ortega, president of Nicaragua

used to back other Central American revolutions, so instead it offered to provide training and army medical units to work in rural areas.

The Sandinistas rejected both suggestions. They pointed out that more officers from the Guardia Nacional than from any other Latin American army had passed through U.S. military schools, so they had reason to distrust American training. As for the medical teams, the FSLN suspected that they might be staffed by CIA operatives. The Sandinistas turned to France for weapons, but the French wanted cash, and Washington lobbied against the sales; that source was soon closed. In 1980 they managed to obtain some Soviet-built tanks from Algeria, but finally it was the Kremlin that became Nicaragua's major military supplier.

By mid-1980 the Sandinista Popular Army probably numbered 13,000 to 18,000 troops. Between 60,000 and 100,000 volunteer part-time militias had also received some rudimentary training.[6] This early concern with the armed forces was born of the conviction that the United States would sooner or later attempt to overthrow the revolution. In 1979 Humberto Ortega discounted the possibility of a direct U.S. invasion, but he warned that "the North Americans will use other means of struggle to displace the hegemony of Sandinism. They will move in economically and politically, trying to foster ideological divisions."[7] For that reason the FSLN made no apologies for its determination to politicize the army. "There are no apolitical armies: every one serves some determinant political purpose," Tomas Borge argued.[8]

The Break

Meanwhile relations with the domestic opposition again began to break down. In early March the Junta passed decrees imposing stiff penalties for decapitalization (withdrawal and flight abroad of investments) and announced that all lands illegally occupied by peasants would be nationalized with compensation. COSEP particularly feared the decapitalization decree, and for the first time Robelo began to criticize the FSLN publicly, accusing it of deviating from the Plan of Government.

In 1978 the Burgeses and the Sandinistas had entered into a marriage of convenience, united only by their opposition to Somoza. It had been a shotgun wedding in the shadow of the insurrection. The honeymoon lasted nine months and the divorce came on April 21st, when the Junta announced the revised composition of the Council of State. From the original proposed body of thirty-three members it had been expanded to forty-seven, of which an automatic majority of twenty-four seats went to Sandinista organizations: six for the FSLN, nine for the CDSs, six to the two Sandinista unions, one for the armed forces, and one each to the Sandinista women's group and youth group.

The right-of-center opposition was allocated eleven seats: six for COSEP, one for Robelo's party—the MDN—and one each for the Social Christian Party, the Conservative Party, the Social Christian trade union (CTN), and an independent trade union (CUS). Three other parties—the Independent Liberals, the Popular Social Christians, and the Socialists—were allocated one seat each, and they quickly formed a voting coalition with the Sandinistas called the Patriotic Revolutionary Front. On the Left, the Socialist Party's trade union was given two seats and the Communist trade union was given one. Catholic priests had one representative, as did the Indian tribes from the Atlantic coast. The rest went to independent trade unions.

Although the number of seats assigned to the middle-class opposition was almost certainly more than they could have won in elections at that time, it was far less than they had anticipated, and it ensured Sandinista dominance. The next day Robelo accused the FSLN of breaking the national consensus. He resigned from the Junta and called on the opposition parties to boycott the Council of State. The Sandinistas counterattacked, accusing Robelo in essence of being a selfish, greedy millionaire who cared nothing for the poor.

Yet, at the same time they moved quickly to paper over the divisions with COSEP through a series of secretly negotiated concessions. They agreed to lift the state of emergency that had been in effect since the Triumph and to restore *habeas corpus;* they guaranteed the freedom of the private radio stations; and they promised to announce dates for general and municipal elections on July 19, 1980. After lengthy discussions with the U.S. embassy, COSEP finally agreed to take up its seats in the council. A top COSEP member, José Francisco Cardenal, was elected a vice president of the council. But Cardenal denounced his appointment as "a hellish conspiracy of the Communist machine," resigned his post and fled to the United States, where he immediately set to work to raise a force of anti-Sandinista guerrillas.[9] For their part the MDN, the Conservatives and the Social Christians did boycott the assembly for several weeks. It was evidence of the continuing divisions among the traditional parties.

It also demonstrated that many Burgeses were not prepared to accept a secondary role to the FSLN. In essence it was a microcosm of the long-running constitutional crisis that would lead Nicaragua back to war. For a pluralist society to function there must be a minimum of consensus among the most powerful political forces; they must at least accept the major institutions of state as a framework within which to operate. Republicans and Democrats in the U.S., for example, may differ over policy, but they accept the division of powers between Congress and the executive branch, and the methods by which they are chosen. In Nicaragua many Burgeses refused to accept the parliament (the Council of State); they did not accept the army; they did not even accept the judiciary.

Instead of staying in the country and working within these structures to change the government peacefully, they left Nicaragua and worked for the violent overthrow of the revolution, arguing that they had no other option because of the extent of Sandinista power. The Sandinistas countered that the opposition never seriously tried democratic methods and that subsequent restrictions of political and individual rights were a consequence, not a cause, of the war. The argument continues to this day, both inside Nicaragua and in the U.S. Congress.

Divided Right

Three days before Robelo's resignation, Violeta de Chamorro had also quit the Junta, for health reasons. Suddenly the Junta was bereft of any representatives from the traditional parties. Robelo later admitted that he had hoped this would provoke a political crisis and force the Sandinistas to make major concessions such as power-sharing with the Right.[10] But the plan foundered on the continuing inability of the opposition to agree on tactics: on May 18th the FSLN nominated two Conservative leaders to replace Chamorro and Robelo, and both men gladly accepted. The new Junta members were the Central Bank president Arturo Cruz and a prominent lawyer, Rafael Cordova Rivas. "Political pluralism has been maintained," Cordova Rivas said in his acceptance speech. Nevertheless many of Robelo's supporters resigned from the bureaucracy, further weakening opposition influence inside the government.

Meanwhile the opposition newspaper, *La Prensa*, was paralyzed by a political dispute between members of the Chamorro family. The editor, Xavier Chamorro, brother of the assassinated Pedro Joaquin Chamorro, objected to the bitter anti-Sandinista columns being written by Pedro Joaquin's son. On April 20th Xavier was dismissed by other family members, and the workers struck. COSEP and Violeta de Chamorro blamed the Sandinistas, but the FSLN helped mediate a solution. Xavier quit, taking with him most of the journalists and print workers. He founded a new newspaper called *Nuevo Diario* which was critical but supportive of the Sandinistas.

July 19, 1980, marked the first anniversary of the Nicaraguan revolution. In Managua a crowd estimated by several sources at 500,000 people gathered for a celebration. The guests were a mixed bunch: Felipe Gonzalez, who would become prime minister of Spain in 1982; the vice president of the Supreme Soviet; the U.S. ambassador to the United Nations; the prime ministers of Grenada and Belize; the former presidents of Costa Rica and Venezuela; and two days later the chairman of the PLO, Yasir Arafat, would also arrive. But on that hot, festive afternoon all eyes were fixed on the Cuban leader, Fidel Castro. With his trademark cigar poking from his bushy beard, he beamed down at the Sandinista leaders clustered around him. Many reporters commented that he looked like a father-figure surrounded by adoring children. It was exactly the sort of image that set teeth grinding in Washington.

The Sandinistas reviewed their troops. Daniel Ortega made a speech and announced that large farms that were not being efficiently managed would be expropriated. There was no announcement of election dates as promised, which outraged the opposition.

Revolutionary Elections

On August 23rd, at another huge demonstration of more than a quarter of a million people, Humberto Ortega rectified the omission. He said that an election would be held in 1985. But, Ortega warned, "Our elections will be to perfect revolutionary power, not to hold a raffle among those who seek to hold power, because the people hold power through their vanguard—the FSLN and its National Directorate." Ortega also promised that "the elections we speak of are very different from the elections desired by the oligarchs and traitors, Conservatives and Liberals, reactionaries and imperialists."[11]

COSEP and the opposition parties were horrified. They had hoped for a much earlier test at the ballot box; in fact it had been their last hope for a greater share of power, and they did not like the sound of this new type of election. The problems of capital flight worsened. In the mountains the remnants of the Guardia stepped up their attacks. Food shortages occurred. Some were the result of the agricultural disruption during the previous year's fighting, but the FSLN blamed deliberate economic sabotage engineered by COSEP using scare stories in *La Prensa*—the paper had indeed predicted a sugar shortage, which caused some panic buying. In early September the Junta reacted: it issued decrees forbidding newspapers to print "disinformation" about the economy and security matters. It was a first taste of censorship. The decrees also banned electioneering until 1984. Meanwhile Sandinista leaders started to publicly suggest that middle-class opponents were organizing an "internal counter-revolutionary movement."[12]

Plotting

More businessmen left the country. Many of those who remained felt that there was no longer anything to be gained from cooperating with the FSLN. They decided it was time for a showdown; Robelo called a mass MDN demonstration for November 9, 1980, just five days after Ronald Reagan had been elected president of the United States. The Interior Ministry said it had evidence that armed counter-revolutionaries planned to infiltrate the march and asked Robelo to cancel it. He refused, so the Junta banned the demonstration under the new decree outlawing election campaigns. But on November 9th gangs of Sandinista supporters were allowed to gather outside MDN offices around the country. They ransacked the MDN headquarters in Managua while the police stood by and refused to intervene. In response the COSEP delegates walked out of the Council of State, abandoning yet another platform from which to oppose the FSLN democratically.

But by then another opposition figure, Jorge Salazar, had decided on a more radical approach. Salazar was one of

COSEP's top leaders. He was a charismatic and popular figure who headed an organization of 7,000 coffee farmers. Like Robelo he had the potential to become a major national political figure. But in May 1980, even before the start of censorship or restrictions on political activity, he decided to organize a coup d'état and overthrow the Sandinistas. He plotted with disaffected Sandinista army officers, with José Francisco Cardenal in the United States, and with right wing generals in El Salvador who provided weapons. He also invited Robelo to join his group. Robelo refused but did not tell the authorities about the plot. They soon found out anyway.

On November 17, 1980, Salazar was shot by uniformed Sandinista security agents outside a gas station. They said they had gone to arrest him and that he had been caught in crossfire when his accomplice started shooting at them. COSEP members claimed he had been deliberately enticed into the plot and shot in cold blood so that the Sandinistas could dispose of a popular opponent. On November 19 the FSLN decided to squash those allegations with a show of support; some 100,000 people took to the streets. Clearly the FSLN still commanded immense popular backing.

Although more Burgeses abandoned the country, many still remained, and the Carter administration appropriated $1 million in secret funds to strengthen the opposition parties.[13] But after November the focus shifted away from a political struggle for power to the armed attempt to overthrow the revolution. The reason for the change was to be found 2,000 miles to the north in Washington, D.C.

Ronald Reagan

As he campaigned for the presidency, Ronald Reagan had insisted that it was time, once more, for the United States to carry a big stick. The Republican platform stated: "We deplore the Marxist Sandinista takeover of Nicaragua and the Marxist attempts to destabilize El Salvador, Guatemala, and Honduras. We will return to the fundamental principle of treating a friend as a friend and self-proclaimed enemies as enemies, without apology." The platform approved by the Republican convention in July warned that "the Soviet Union and its surrogates operate by a far different set of rules than does the United States," including "terrorism." While a Reagan administration would not copy those tactics, the convention delegates were told, it would use covert action and other intelligence activities.

What made the Sandinistas really worried, though, was the Republicans' vow to cut aid to Nicaragua and to "support the efforts of the Nicaraguan people to establish a free and independent government." The FSLN immediately concluded that this meant support for an armed rebellion and a CIA plot to overthrow their government. From that moment they started to prepare. Their preparations included a resolve to control the domestic opposition so that the CIA could not use it to destabilize society, as had happened in Iran in 1953 and Chile in 1973. In fact by then several businessmen were already in the pay of the CIA.[14]

But Sandinista plans were not only defensive. During the first anniversary celebrations a delegation from the El Salvadoran guerrilla movement had been in Nicaragua. The Left had suffered enormously in El Salvador in the months after the Sandinista victory, as the army there moved to prevent a repetition of the Nicaraguan experience. Thousands of trade unionists, human rights activists, student leaders, and politicians had been tortured, gunned down, and "disappeared" by right-wing death squads. The Salvadoran guerrillas had given the Sandinistas money and fighters in the last months of the insurrection, now they called in their marker. In the early fall the Sandinistas gave them some ammunition and guns. The Carter administration found out and told the Sandinistas to stop, which they did. But when Reagan was elected, they decided that it was worth the gamble—a second revolutionary government in Central America would provide moral support—so they bet that they could present Reagan with a *fait accompli* before the inauguration. On January 10, 1981, the Salvadorans launched a "final offensive" with tons of weapons shipped through Nicaragua. Within days the offensive collapsed. The gamble had failed, and Sandinista involvement had been exposed.

As soon as he took office Reagan cut all Nicaraguan aid, including food supplies. By March the Sandinistas had allowed the secret Salvadoran arms pipeline to run dry.[15] Ambassador Pezzullo believed that the Sandinistas had proved that they would relent in the face of clearly and forcefully expressed U.S. security concerns. He recommended resuming aid, to give the administration a tool to use in further negotiations. But the White House rejected that idea. Instead on March 9, 1981, Reagan signed a secret "finding"—a presidential authorization for CIA operations in Nicaragua.[16] It was the start of U.S. backing for the counter-revolutionaries, known to everyone as the Contras, who were trying to overthrow the Sandinistas.

SEVEN

THE BIRTH OF THE CONTRAS

The Sandinistas are political crusaders. To understand the bitterness of the conflict with the United States, it is important to understand that from the start of the Reagan administration in 1981 U.S. policy in Central America was also directed by political crusaders. The Reagan administration marked the first time that the conservative wing of the Republican Party had occupied the White House. The conservatives were fierce anti-Communists who believed that the world was inexorably becoming dominated by the Soviet Union. They believed that the U.S. could have won the Vietnam war and that the troops were betrayed by liberals in the media and Congress. Many of those involved in President Reagan's Central American policy were veterans of Vietnam—marine vets, CIA vets, and diplomatic vets—men such as Lieutenant Colonel Oliver North, Thomas Enders, and Major General Richard Secord. They were determined to challenge Soviet power and above all to "roll back" a Communist state as a demonstration of U.S. resolve. Early on Nicaragua became the testing ground for the rollback theory, and right-wing lobbyists were pushing for a military response to the Sandinistas even before the new administration took office.

President Reagan himself saw Nicaragua as a symbol in his ideological war with the Kremlin. As he said in one speech, failure to support the Contras would send "an unmistakable signal that the greatest power in the world is unwilling and incapable of stopping Communist aggression in our own backyard."[1] Compromise with the Sandinistas was out of the question, they had to be kicked out of power to make an example. In "Banana Diplomacy"—an exhaustive study of relations between the Reagan White House and the Nicaraguan Comandantes—author Roy Gutman shows how hard-line right-wingers in the administration successfully blocked all efforts at a negotiated solution with the Sandinistas and indeed provoked the Sandinistas to become more repressive to justify an escalating military response.[2]

Many Congressmen were unconvinced of the strategic threat that the White House said the Sandinistas represented, and unwilling to get into "another Vietnam." So democracy became the stated goal of U.S. policy but, as Gutman says, "democracy ... came to stand for overthrow of the regime." The tool to achieve that overthrow was to be the Contras.

U.S. Money, Argentine Training, Nicaraguan Bodies

The Contras started to organize on the very day of the Triumph, when a phony Red Cross plane, piloted by an American mercenary, flew into Managua to evacuate top Guardia officers. Over the next few days he rounded up about 130 Guardias and took them back to Miami where they started to plot.[3]

Other Guardias formed small bands operating on the Honduran border or deep in the Jinotega mountains. These groups were made up of privates and sergeants; those who did not have the money or the contacts to get to the United States. They had few skills and little knowledge of anything except fighting, so they chose to bury themselves in the jungle and to live like bandits. They were fired by a hatred of the Sandinistas and by a yearning to somehow restore the Somoza regime, but they had no clear political program. During the Literacy Crusade they killed several teachers and militiamen in a series of uncoordinated actions.

By early 1980 Tachito's cousin, Luis Pallais Debayle, was spending hundreds of thousands of dollars trying to organize these diverse Guardia remnants. Somoza himself promised a million dollars, but before he could deliver, on September 17th, he and his car were blown to smithereens by a left-wing Argentine hit squad in Paraguay in a show of "solidarity" with the FSLN. But the organizing continued and a leadership evolved, composed entirely of "Somocistas," figures linked to the Somoza dictatorship. Despite later infusions of people who were less politically compromised, the Somocista legacy was to dog the Contras and their search for political credibility.

Despite the convictions of the Reagan team, the early Contra policy was shaped more by outsiders and freelancers than by the White House. In March 1981 the new army-appointed Argentine president, General Gustavo Viola, visited Washington where conservative lobbyists encouraged him to back the Contras. In April the military strongman in Honduras, Colonel Gustavo Alvarez Martinez, met the CIA director William Casey and proposed a guerrilla war against the Sandinistas launched from Honduran territory and designed to provoke a Sandinista response that might justify a U.S. invasion. Meanwhile a U.S. Army officer, Major General Robert Laurence Schweitzer, traveled to Honduras and on his own initiative urged the Contras to organize. Between these disparate elements a plan started to emerge. As one Contra leader described it to the author, "the U.S. puts up the money, the Argentines put up the training, and the Nicas put up the bodies."

In May 1981, with $50,000 from the CIA, Argentine military officers started to train and arm 1,000 Contras in Honduras. In August, with CIA help, the different Guardia factions united and christened themselves the Nicaraguan Democratic Force (FDN). They chose a former Guardia colonel, Enrique Bermudez, as their leader. That month Duane "Dewey" Clarridge, the chief of the CIA's Latin American section, visited the Honduran capital, Tegucigalpa, where he told the Honduran army high command that he had been personally sent by the president and that the United States would support guerrilla action to "liberate" Nicaragua.4 It was not exactly true. Nevertheless by the summer of 1981 Nicaraguan exiles were training in the Florida Everglades.

There was one last try at diplomacy before the FDN swung into action. In August 1981, the assistant secretary of state for inter-American affairs, Thomas Enders, visited Managua and threatened the Sandinistas with intervention. He offered a deal: normal relations with the U.S. if the FSLN agreed to halt aid to other revolutionaries in El Salvador, Honduras, Guatemala, and Costa Rica. Despite their outrage at the tone of the talks, the Sandinistas agreed. But back in Washington Enders was severely criticized by hardliners for not pressing for "democratization." In September joint U.S.-Honduran military maneuvers started north of the border. They were meant to scare the Sandinistas and they did. From then on U.S. maneuvers in Honduras were to become a regular feature and a constant reminder of the weight of U.S. military power.

Against this backdrop Enders stiffened his demands. Arturo Cruz, who by then had become ambassador to Washington, described the Enders position as insulting, like "the conditions of a victorious power."5 The talks collapsed. In November 1981 the president approved nearly $20 million in support of the Argentine operation in Honduras. In December Congress gave the green light, but restricted the activity to arms "interdiction."

On March 14, 1982, a CIA-trained team of Contra saboteurs blew up two important bridges in northern Nicaragua. It marked the start of the war, and the Sandinistas reacted the next day by declaring a state of emer-

Early photo of the leaders of the FDN (the Contras) holding a press conference

gency. Within days Alfonso Robelo went into self-imposed exile. He was followed by most of the top MDN members, which left the opposition in Nicaragua weaker than ever. There had been other departures. Earlier, in November 1981, Arturo Cruz had resigned from his job as ambassador to Washington and quit the Sandinistas; he voiced no criticism at the time but was upset at the Sandinistas' increasing harassment of private businessmen.

The Southern Front

Before Cruz resigned there had been an even more significant loss. In July 1981, Eden Pastora had quit. Pastora was a Sandinista hero and the popular commander of the 1978 National Palace raid. He left Nicaragua out of a mixture of boredom, disgust at his lowly position as deputy defense minister, and unhappiness about the political direction of the revolution. At first he said he was going to fight other revolutions, and he briefly flirted with the Guatemalan guerrillas. Then he decided to fight his former comrades in the FSLN. For several months in mid-1982 the CIA tried to persuade him to unite with the FDN, but Pastora thought them too tainted with "Somocismo," and they thought him too left-wing. In addition Commander Zero, as Pastora was widely known, insisted that he should have overall command. This was too much for the Somocistas, who in any case thought Pastora was an unstable egomaniac. Finally Commander Zero and Robelo announced the creation of the Revolutionary Democratic Alliance (ARDE) based in Costa Rica, and in April 1983 ARDE went on the attack.

The Contra Invasion

At the end of 1982 the CIA selected six civilians to form a new Directorate of the FDN in an effort to dilute the Somocista cast of characters. They were presented to the press. One was Adolfo Calero, a businessman and Conservative Party leader who had remained in Nicaragua until December, ostensibly as a leader of the opposition. It later emerged that Calero had been working for the CIA for several years.[6] Another of the civilians was Edgar Chamorro: "The CIA chose us, they organized the press conference, and they told us what to say," Chamorro later told the author. "They also promised to help us capture Managua within six months. All we had to do was follow CIA orders."

Between the demolition of the bridges in March 1982 and the appointment of the new FDN Directorate at the end of that year, there had been little fighting in Nicaragua: a few cross-border attacks and a big assault on the northern border town of Jalapa. But by late Spring 1983 the FDN had infiltrated between 2,000 and 4,000 men deep inside the country.

The FDN quickly acquired a reputation for brutality. For the most part they steered clear of military targets.

Instead, for the next six years they went after civilian targets. According to published statistics, by July 1986 the Contras had destroyed fifty-eight schools, twenty-nine health clinics, eleven childcare centers, and dozens of agricultural cooperatives.[7] The tactics would not change throughout the fighting. Like their conservative supporters in Washington, the Contra leaders were much clearer about what they were against than what they were for. They attacked Sandinista public works projects, such as schools, precisely because the Sandinistas had built them. It is little surprise they never won much support inside the country. In 1986 a congressional report would conclude that "The Nicaraguan Resistance remains without a political infrastructure inside Nicaragua or a clear political message to give to the Nicaraguan people. It has never developed urban support. In fact, years of United States assistance have not produced an insurgency capable of sustaining itself among the population in Nicaragua."[8]

But back in 1983 the Sandinistas were slow to respond to the Contras, and for the next two years volunteer militias and reserve battalions carried the brunt of the fighting. It was a time when the Sandinistas genuinely feared that they might be militarily overthrown. They tried to anticipate all sorts of scenarios involving combinations of Contra attacks, military incursions by troops from Central American neighbors, a U.S. invasion, and internal sabotage by Contra sympathizers. The Reagan administration did its best to foster these fears and to provoke the Sandinistas to clamp down on their political opposition, in the hope that this would cause discontent in Nicaragua and provide ammunition with which to attack the Sandinistas on the international diplomatic front.

Invasion Fears

In March 1983 the Contras launched a major assault in an attempt to capture the northern border town of Jalapa. In May, General Paul Gorman, the new head of the U.S. Southern Command in Panama, started to draw up detailed invasion plans. In July the aircraft carrier *Ranger* and its battle group appeared off the coast of Nicaragua. In September thousands of U.S. troops started fresh maneuvers in Honduras, the largest such operation ever seen in Central America. At the same time the battle cruiser *New Jersey* steamed off the Pacific coast. In September and October high-speed motorboats manned by CIA-hired operatives attacked oil installations at Corinto and Puerto Sandino.9 The second attack on Corinto forced the evacuation of 25,000 civilians for fear that some fuel tanks might explode; the blaze lasted for two days. Over the next six months CIA teams were used on at least five occasions to mount air attacks against selected targets in Nicaragua. In October military officers from El Salvador, Honduras, Guatemala, and Panama discussed the possibility of joint intervention in Nicaragua in the event that the Contras could "liberate" some territory and form a provisional government. Meanwhile the CIA started to send fake radio signals intended to convince the FSLN that an invasion might be in the offing.

It worked; the Sandinistas were worried. But after the U.S. invasion of Grenada on October 25th, they panicked. For a while they seriously believed Nicaragua might be next. Volunteers started digging trenches all over Managua; the TV was flooded with ads teaching people how to shoot a rifle and the correct way to build an air-raid shelter; supermarket shelves were stripped bare; even Western embassies discussed evacuation plans. In November, in an effort to prove their reasonableness, the FSLN ordered the Salvadoran guerrillas to dismantle their high command and leave the country, and Daniel Ortega said 1,000 Cuban advisers would be sent back to Havana. Censorship was suddenly relaxed. Elections were announced for 1985. Finally the Sandinistas submitted a draft treaty to the Contadora Group (Colombia, Mexico, Panama, and Venezuela), which since January had been trying to find a negotiated solution to all the regional problems. The treaty offered major concessions on elections and U.S. security concerns.

It seemed to be a great opportunity to resolve the problems between the two countries. President Reagan's special envoy to Central America, former Senator Richard Stone, hoped to do just that and planned to negotiate with the Sandinistas. But the hard-line conservatives inside the administration were adamantly opposed to any agreement that would endanger the existence of the Contras. In addition, no one inside the administration seemed clear about what specifically they wanted to achieve in Nicaragua, short of the total expulsion of the Sandinistas. Meanwhile, behind the scenes, there was a power struggle for control of Central American policy between Stone and Langhorne Anthony Motley, Enders's replacement as assistant secretary of state for inter-American affairs. In February 1984 Motley won, Stone resigned, and with him went the hopes for a negotiated settlement. Once again the ideologues in Washington had prevailed and diplomacy never stood a chance.[10]

The year 1984 marked the high point of the Contras' fortunes. The Sandinistas had not yet put together an effective counter-insurgency effort, and their only tactic was to throw large numbers of untrained and inexperienced militiamen into the field in an effort to keep the Contras on the move. Against trained former Guardias the militia were cannon-fodder, and the Sandinistas suffered heavy casualties.

The Contra successes enabled them to recruit many more men. It is impossible to know accurately how many guerrillas the FDN was able to field at any one time because, as would be revealed during Congressional hearings in 1987, the CIA and the State Department exaggerated the FDN numbers for propaganda purposes. The best estimate is that at their height FDN may have been able to field 15,000 men. The majority of these fighters were peasants.

Obviously not all of them were ex-Guardias or even Somoza supporters. So why did they join the Contras? Some of them joined because of mistreatment by the Sandinistas. In the early days several young FSLN guerrilla commanders who were suddenly given authority in remote mountain villages behaved in a high-handed way, confiscating farms and jailing people without trial. (See the Barquero case in Chapter Eight.) Others joined out of fear. The author has interviewed several Contras who had been told by FDN officers that the Sandinistas would not allow them to practice their religion or that their farms would be seized for cooperatives. Some were recruited with offers of good pay and decent uniforms. Some, according to the Sandinistas, were kidnapped and forced to fight. For whatever reason, between 1983 and 1984 the FDN numbers grew more rapidly than the Sandinistas had ever anticipated was possible, and for a while they thought the Contras might be able to seize a remote piece of territory and form a provisional government.

Mining the Harbors

But then in January 1984 the CIA committed a major gaffe. CIA contract teams laid mines in Nicaragua's three largest ports. Britain called it a "threat to the principle of freedom of navigation." France offered to send minesweepers to clear the sea lanes. Senator Barry Goldwater, chairman of the Intelligence Committee and one of the most conservative members of Congress, complained that his committee had not been informed and that the mining went far beyond "interdiction" of weapons to the Salvadoran guerrillas.

The operation ultimately led Congress to totally suspend aid to the Contras in October 1984. In the meantime, in April, the Sandinistas filed suit at the World Court, forcing the United States into the embarrassing position of having to withdraw from the court to avoid a widely anticipated defeat. (In June 1986 the United States would be found guilty of violating international law, a ruling backed by fourteen out of the fifteen judges, including those from Britain, France, Italy, West Germany, and Japan.) Finally, the mining-inspired aid cut-off would also lead to the "Iran-Contra affair," which undermined the Reagan administration's authority in Congress for its last two years, hampered White House policies, and caused the president's popularity to plummet.

The mining fracas was a setback to the ideologues in the administration and allowed the State department to try diplomacy once more. During 1983 Secretary of State George Shultz had been so frozen out of Nicaraguan policy that he offered to resign,[11] but in June 1984 he swung into action; he visited Managua and initiated a series of nine rounds of bilateral talks held in Manzanillo, Mexico. In Washington the conservatives were busy again trying to block a negotiated solution. For their part the Sandinistas did not realize that the pro-Contra forces in Washington had been dealt a setback, leaving room for some real advance. They thought the talks were a pre-election propaganda ploy as Ronald Reagan prepared for his campaign to win a second term in the White House. They did not seize the opportunity to press for peace.

Part of the reason was that by then the Sandinistas were convinced that nothing they could do would satisfy the United States. Every aspect of their government was attacked by the White House, even the advances in education and health care of which they were so proud. President Reagan himself consistently accused the Sandinistas of being totalitarian Communists. He found evidence for this in three major areas: violations of basic human and political rights; a Marxist economy; and repression of religion.

EIGHT

HUMAN RIGHTS

One day in November 1983 five bullet-ridden bodies were dumped on the road on the edge of the dusty village of Pantasma in northern Nicaragua. When the news reached the authorities forty miles away in the regional capital, Jinotega, they decided to investigate. They did not like what they found. The murderer turned out to be the senior Sandinista official in Pantasma, Carlos José Barquero. Following a Contra attack on Pantasma that had left thirty-two civilians and fifteen soldiers dead, Barquero had launched a campaign of terror against anyone he suspected of being anti-Sandinista. In thirteen weeks Barquero and his men had murdered six civilians, tortured four, and raped at least one woman. Four other people had disappeared. He had also confiscated seventeen farms, stolen cattle and trucks, and beaten local *campesinos* (peasants).[1]

It was deeply embarrassing. Barquero had what the FSLN called a *trayectoria* (a history of exemplary conduct). He was a politicized factory worker who had fought bravely in the insurrection. Nevertheless the Sandinistas decided to make an example. He and forty-one of his men were arrested and tried before dozens of *campesinos* specially trucked in from Pantasma, so that justice could be seen to be done. Twenty-nine soldiers were acquitted, but Barquero was sentenced to forty-four years in jail and thirteen others received a range of prison terms. "What makes us different from the enemy," boasted the civil governor of Jinotega province, Juan José Ubeda, "is the firmness to energetically punish crimes including those committed by our own people."[2] By "enemy" Ubeda meant the Contras and the U.S.-backed military regimes in the region: El Salvador, Guatemala, and Honduras. By "crimes" he meant the most basic and outrageous of human-rights abuses: murder, physical torture, and rape.

The Sandinista Definition of Human Rights

The Reagan administration has helped focus human rights in Nicaragua under the glare of media attention, forcing Nicaragua to live up to a standard that successive administrations had never demanded of the Somoza dictatorship.

At first the record was quite impressive. In the confusion immediately after the Triumph, there was no "Red Terror." Some people seized the opportunity to settle accounts, some Somocistas were killed and others arrested on flimsy evidence,[3] but most human rights groups accepted that the FSLN had not endorsed these actions and they were quickly curbed. At the same time Borge pointed out that young and inexperienced guerrilla leaders would need time to learn the more difficult job of being bureaucrats and policemen.

Some early moves were internationally applauded: the death penalty was abolished and the Sandinistas introduced an open prison system for some prisoners, which is still a model for the rest of the region. These prisoners receive visits by their spouses, and good behavior allows them to progress through a series of increasingly lenient regimes until eventually they are allowed out all day, to work unsupervised cultivating farmland provided by the government. They are allowed to keep the profits from sales of their produce.

Other actions in the first year drew a more mixed response. The FSLN was praised for ensuring that there were no mass executions of Somocista prisoners and for promising a fair trial to all 6,330 captured Guardias. But then the Junta argued that it could not use the normal court system, because it would take years to hear every case. Instead special tribunals were created. Human-rights groups complained that these did not guarantee a fair trial. Nevertheless, 1,999 Guardias were soon released for lack of evidence, while 4331 were convicted of what might be called war crimes. By 1988 2,499 of those had served their sentences and been released, leaving 1,832 in jail.[4] In early 1989 the Sandinistas agreed to release all remaining Guardias as part of a regional peace accord.

Despite the good start it quickly became apparent that the Sandinistas had a broader view of human rights than their middle-class opposition. "For us the most important human rights are the right to a roof over your head, the right to health care and education, the right to a job," said Tomas Borge. "What does freedom of speech mean to a man who is starving?"[5]

The Sandinistas believed they had a duty, as the "vanguard" of the people, to satisfy and defend those rights. They also believed that the best defense was to prevent the revolutionary government from being overthrown by the Contras: if that meant sacrificing civil or political rights, so be it.

The Early Years

As we have seen, in the spring of 1982 the American media revealed that President Reagan had approved CIA plans to help the Contras, and on March 14 the Contras blew up two important bridges. The Junta responded the next day by declaring a state of emergency, which suspended most civil rights, including habeas corpus and protection from arbitrary search and seizure. These moves allowed the police to arrest people merely on suspicion and to hold prisoners incommunicado for long periods of time. Opposition radio news broadcasts were halted and prior censorship introduced for all newspapers and magazines. The Universal Declaration of Human Rights contains a clause which allows the suspension of civil liberties in the face of direct military threats, and as international law requires, the Junta wrote to the UN Secretary General giving the reasons for their action.[6]

The Sandinistas argued that the measures were needed to prevent Contra sympathizers inside the country from conducting sabotage, recruiting supporters, and destabilizing the government by organizing strikes or protests. They insisted the emergency powers were similar to those used by the United States during both world wars to jail pacifists, to ban radical publications, and to hold thousands of Japanese-Americans in internment camps.[7] Critics argued that the restrictions were not justified by the war and were merely a convenient excuse to mask the Sandinistas' classic Leninist intentions to repress the democratic opposition and create a one-party state.

Indeed the Sandinistas had shown disregard of some civil rights before the Contras became a major threat. For example, in June 1980 hundreds of what the police claimed were potential troublemakers were arrested in advance of the arrival of important guests for the first anniversary celebrations. Not only were they not brought to court within the required 24-hour period, but several were kept in illegal detention for weeks. In January 1980 leaders of the ultra-left Workers Front were sentenced to jail under Public Order laws, but in May it became convenient to release them to win left-wing support, so the FSLN simply ignored the courts and set them free. Also, the Supreme Court complained several times that its decisions were not promptly obeyed.

The Reagan administration claimed these abuses were

early evidence that the FSLN was dictatorial and would not allow free political activity to challenge its power, thereby justifying an armed response. The Sandinistas say they were temporary special measures required during the period of instability after the Triumph. In fact in an overview of Nicaragua's human rights record published by Amnesty International, there is little evidence of a pattern of abuse before the Contras became a major force.[8]

In practice the international criticism of the Sandinistas on human rights has focused on three areas that all started to receive attention after the onset of the Contra war in 1982. The first area covers arbitrary arrests, degrading jail conditions, and psychological torture to extract confessions. The second criticism is of unfairly conducted trials, at which some suspects have been allegedly jailed for their political views. The third area is censorship.

Arbitrary Arrests

Shortly after the Triumph the Interior Ministry created the Dirección General de Seguridad de Estado (DGSE), the secret police. It was organized with help from Cuba, and the opposition was quick to label it a Nicaraguan KGB. With increasing frequency after March 1982, the DGSE arrested opposition businessmen, trade unionists, and politicians. Often they would be seized from their homes late at night. They were taken to El Chipote interrogation center, the only prison in Nicaragua not open to Red Cross inspection. According to Amnesty International the cells in El Chipote are cramped, badly lit, and unventilated. Detainees are often kept in solitary confinement, the food is inadequate, prisoners are sometimes deprived of sleep, and they or their families are physically threatened. There have also been several reports of beatings. Often the prisoners are held for months and then released without charges, and Amnesty International believes this whole procedure may be "in order to harass sections of the legal opposition."[9]

But as Amnesty International admits, some of the detainees have been suspected of "involvement with armed opposition groups," and as Jorge Salazar's early coup attempt proved, not all those who claim to be democrats reject violent methods. Indeed several businessmen have told the author "off the record" that they would be happy to see the Contras win: "I went to school with their leaders, we are friends, I know them and I know I can trust them to be good democrats if they win," one said. "Of course I would be enchanted if the Contras triumphed," another said. "But in reality I think Reagan should send in the marines, the sooner the better."

As recently as September 1988 the Speaker of the House of Representatives, Jim Wright, revealed that the CIA was involved with the domestic opposition in an attempt to provoke a violent reaction from the government.[10] The Sandinistas, aware of this, believe all the Burgeses are potential agents of the Contras. As Marxists, the Sandinistas are convinced that class interests will prevail and that the middle classes are all natural allies of the Contras. For that reason they have tended to lump all the Burgeses into the same bag, and whether or not they have reason to suspect individuals of complicity, they periodically arrest or harass all the top opposition leaders as a means of "warning" them away from illegal activities. Of course such "warnings" also tend to deter legal, democratic, opposition activities.

But the Sandinistas claim their restrictions do not affect the majority of Nicaraguans. Certainly in Managua and the larger towns there is little climate of fear. People have strong views and are outspoken. During a visit by the author to Managua's largest market, the Mercado Oriental, in 1986, a crowd quickly gathered to express their views. Some were for the revolution, others against. After ten minutes a policeman arrived and hovered on the edges of the crowd. "The Comandantes are all Communists, they have thrown this country down. They should get out," one woman shouted.

"Aren't you afraid to talk like this?" I asked. "No, they won't do anything to me," she answered. However, in the war zones it is more difficult to obtain a reaction, whether this is because of fear of the DGSE or because of the natural reticence of the *campesinos* (peasants) is difficult to gauge.

Nicaragua's Permanent Human Rights Commission is little help in assessing the level of repression since it is politically opposed to the FSLN. As noted earlier, its national coordinator, José Esteban Gonzalez, had tried to prevent a Sandinista victory before the Triumph. For several years its chief legal adviser was Eduardo Rivas Gasteazoro, who was president of the Democratic Coordinator, the major conservative political coalition opposed to the Sandinistas. A second leader of the Permanent Commission, Marta Patricia Baltodano, joined the Contras in 1987. Another group, the Commission for the Promotion and Protection of Human Rights, is equally partial since it was founded and is funded by the government.

Unfair Trials

As the number of captured Contras and suspected Contra sympathizers grew, the courts found themselves unable to handle the case load. The judiciary and the Supreme Court had proved themselves substantially independent of the FSLN and insisted on proper standards of evidence and strict observance of legal procedures. The Junta reacted by creating special courts, the Tribunales Populares Antisomocistas (TPAs), to try so-called Public Order offenses. In November 1987 the TPAs were abolished as part of peace moves. While they operated, the courts were composed of one magistrate with legal training and two lay Sandinista supporters. The Tribunales Populares allowed just two days for preparation of a defense. They had an extremely high conviction rate, often secured solely on the basis of a signed confession, and, despite protests from the Supreme Court, they were outside the normal juridical framework and allowed no appeal to the Supreme Court.

The Tribunales Populares Antisomocistas (TPAs) were special courts set up to try national security offenses. They were criticized for their arbitrary administration of justice and frequent convictions of Sandinista political opponents. Defendant is the former American marine Eugene Hasenfus.

    This system enabled the Sandinistas to jail a large number of opponents. Amnesty International believes many of those convicted have been jailed purely for their political beliefs and has adopted several as "prisoners of conscience."[11] At the end of 1986, according to figures from the Interior Ministry, 777 people had been convicted by the TPAs and another 1,025 were awaiting trial.[12] The Contras and the Reagan administration claimed the number of political prisoners was more than 6,000, but the Americas Watch human rights group said "these figures have no basis."[13]

    The Sandinistas admit the TPAs were far from a perfect legal system, but argue that all governments take exceptional measures in wartime. Dr. Ligia Molina, who presided over the TPAs, also points out that the Tribunales were very similar to the special "Diplock" courts currently used by the British government in Northern Ireland and were better than the system of "Internment"—or detention without trial—the British used in the 1970s. The Diplock courts, named after the official who fashioned them, permit trial before a single judge with no jury, and they accept signed confessions without corroborating evidence from witnesses. Dr. Molina asks, "Why should the North Americans' best ally, with all its wealth and resources, be allowed to use exceptional measures, and Nicaragua, which is poor and fighting the most powerful nation on earth, cannot?"[14]

Censorship

The issue that has gained the most international attention, however, has been censorship, particularly censorship of *La Prensa*. In the first five years of the revolution, *La Prensa* was suspended on seven occasions and failed to publish more than twenty times because censorship was so heavy. In 1987 the paper was banned for fifteen months. In addition editors and journalists have been arrested, harassed, and even jailed. The paper has been starved of newsprint, and the turbas (mobs of Sandinista supporters) have demonstrated violently outside *La Prensa* offices. The censorship has often been petty or absurd, such as banning photos of unpaved streets that might create a bad impression of the revolution. Yet for most of the last nine years *La Prensa* has been able to

Top: Outside the gates of La Prensa. *Since 1979 the paper has opposed the Sandinista government and has been, at times, censored and closed down. Pro-Sandinista grafitti on the walls reads "Down with traitors." Bottom: Jaime Chamorro, current editor of* La Prensa

LA PRENS
SOMOS EL PUEBLO
ORGANIZADO
FUERA LOS TRAIDORES
aniversario
SEGUIRAN
FSLN

LA PRENS
Oposición urge consulta
Se aproximan tres
meses muy críticos

publish highly critical material. As Americas Watch commented in 1986, "What *La Prensa* was actually allowed to publish was the harshest criticism of its own government that could be found in any newspaper in Central America during 1985."[15]

The Reagan administration has argued that freedom of the press is a touchstone of respect for political pluralism and human rights in Nicaragua. As a journalist this author is totally opposed to censorship, but at first sight, it seems odd that *La Prensa* should be given such importance, so much more—for example—than the Tribunales Populares. *La Prensa* is, as even some of its supporters agree, a terrible newspaper. It invents and spreads malicious rumors. In a sensational front-page story in 1985, for example, it reported that a woman had given birth to a live chicken. Even when not censored it very rarely "broke" important stories of Sandinista wrongdoing. In a country of three million where, until recently, more than 50 percent were illiterate, it sells only about 60,000 copies. Most of those are bought by its political supporters on the Right. In other words, it preaches to the converted. So, if the vast majority of Nicaraguans do not rely on it for news, why is it so important?

The answer, according to the Sandinistas, is that *La Prensa* has always been far more than just a newspaper; it has been a political weapon. Pedro Joaquin Chamorro used *La Prensa* to help overthrow the Somozas, as the Sandinistas knew only too well because two of their top leaders worked for it. "We know *La Prensa* is conspiring against us," said one of them, Commander William Ramirez. "I used to be a conspiring journalist myself. What they are trying to do at *La Prensa* we have already done. We know all the tricks."[16] One American expert goes so far as to argue that the main "trick" is to deliberately publish stories that are so outrageous that they compel the government to censor or suspend it, in order to lend fuel to the Reagan administration efforts to overthrow the FSLN.[17] If so, the Sandinistas have blundered into the hands of the CIA on this issue.

The Sandinistas have often accused *La Prensa* of taking CIA money or using CIA propaganda tactics, but no convincing evidence has ever been produced. It is true that the paper has received congressional funds through the National Endowment for Democracy.[18] There is also no question that since at least May 1980 *La Prensa*'s attacks on the Sandinistas have become increasingly strident and have matched the growth in the Contra war.

La Prensa's editors have not disguised their sympathy for the Contras. "Our fight is the same as the FDN's (the largest Contra group)," said Jaime Chamorro, who is the newspaper's editor. "It is like the difference between an infantry and an air force; two arms of the same thing ... A government can be changed only by a conjunction of factors: the military, the international, the diplomatic, the church, the press."[19]

In the end it is impossible to know for certain whether Sandinista actions are motivated by a conviction that *La Prensa* is part of a military-political plot to overthrow the revolution, or whether the Sandinistas simply have a Leninist determination to control the media and crush open expressions of dissent.

Contra Brutality

What is not in doubt is that the vast majority of human rights abuses are a product of the war. By July 1988, according to government figures, 26,527 people had died in the six years of conflict and about 27,000 had been wounded or kidnapped. Of the casualties 9,132 were children.[20] To the embarrassment of the Reagan administration, the Nicaraguans who have been most consistently criticized by human-rights groups for their war record are the Contras.

Amnesty International reported in 1986 that "the number of captives tortured and put to death by FDN forces since 1981 is impossible to determine, but is believed to total several hundred."[21] Americas Watch has regularly reported cases of torture, deliberate attacks on civilians, and executions of unarmed prisoners by the Contras. Some of the torture has been particularly horrific: cutting off genitals, fingers, tongues, and gouging out eyes. The peasant union in Nicaragua told Americas Watch that by 1987 200 farming cooperatives had been attacked and some 1,400 peasants killed. Professionals associated with the Sandinistas have also been favorite targets, including doctors, teachers, and nurses.[22]

The Sandinistas blame the Reagan administration for this abysmal human rights record because the main Contra group was created by, and received a great deal of guidance from, the CIA. As further evidence they point to a manual produced for the Contras in 1984 by the CIA titled "Psychological Operations in Guerrilla Warfare." The manual recommended "neutralizing" civilians who collaborate with the government. This advice caused a furor in Congress, and the House Intelligence Committee concluded that it probably violated the administration's own executive order prohibiting assassination.[23]

The Sandinistas and the White House remained locked in disagreement over the issue of respect for human rights until the very end of the Reagan administration. At his last press conference President Reagan reaffirmed his view that the Sandinistas are "a Communist totalitarian government." In the meantime the conflict has undermined the one area of human rights where the Sandinistas long claimed to have made important advances: living standards, or as Tomas Borge put it, the rights to food, housing, health care, education, and a job.

The war has helped destroy the economy: jobs are being lost; housing, education, and health care are deteriorating; and levels of malnutrition are rapidly rising. The Sandinistas argue that this has been a deliberate tactic by the U.S. and the Contras to undermine their support. The White House and the Contras believe the economy was already doomed by Sandinista mismanagement.

NINE

THE ECONOMY

"Welcome to Nicaragua: Another Diners Club Country." It's the first sign to greet travelers arriving at Managua's international airport. To some it seems incongruous, but in fact forty-three multinational companies continue to operate in Nicaragua, including such American giants as IBM, Texaco, Exxon, John Deere, and Caterpillar. Their presence immediately poses the question, "Does Nicaragua have a Soviet-style economy or not?"

At first sight the answer seems obvious. By 1987 the Nicaraguan economy had collapsed, and on any given morning you could go to a workers' commissary in Managua and see dozens of people lined up to buy a pair of shoes. The shelves in the "People's Supermarkets" were bare but for pots of Bulgarian jam and some collections of Lenin's speeches. There were bread lines outside the bakeries. Putting a meal on the family table had become a headache with frequent shortages of sugar, cooking oil, rice, beans, corn, meat, eggs. Toilet paper and toothpaste were nowhere to be found.

A black market thrived, but vendors who tried to sell scarce products at large profits were liable to be raided by

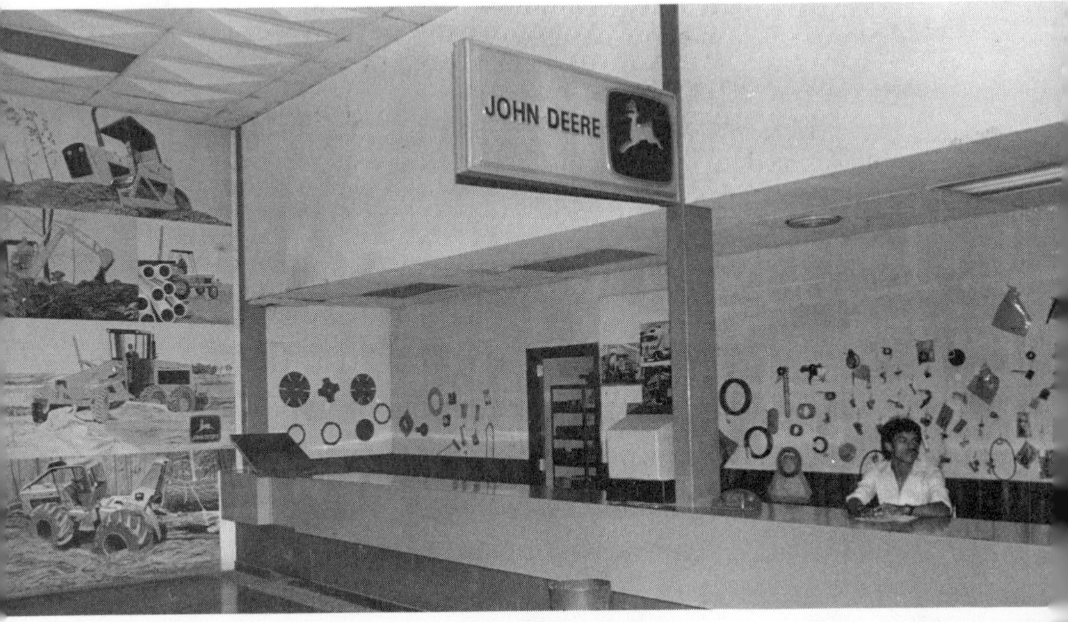
JOHN DEERE

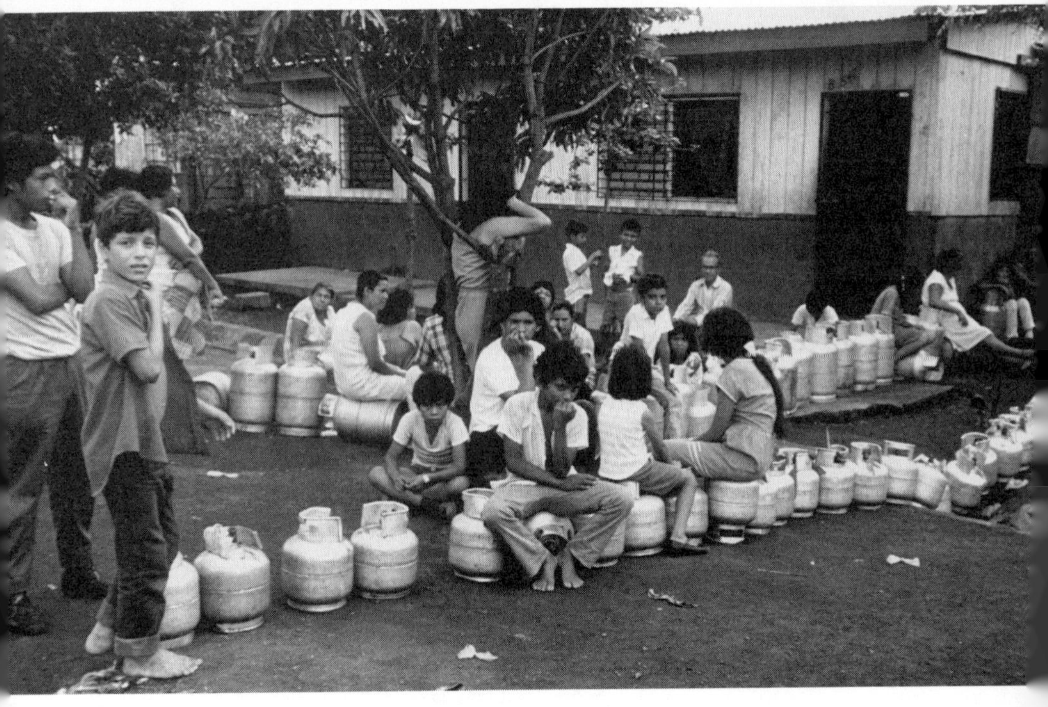

government inspectors. Outside the gas stations lines of cars, hundreds of yards long, built up before dawn as drivers waited patiently to buy rationed gasoline. Water was cut to most sectors of the city twice a week, in some places you were lucky if you had water twice a week. So housewives would get up in the dark to do the family washing before the taps ran dry and pray that the electricity would not be cut again. The only easy way to acquire a car—a Soviet-made Lada—was to find a job as a government bureaucrat. And, to top it all, inflation was running at a crippling 1,300 percent and the foreign debt had reached an incredible $6.7 billion, about $2,000 for every man woman and child. (Brazil, which has the largest foreign debt in Latin America, "only" owes about $900 per person).[1]

The Success of the Early Years

The Reagan administration attitude toward Sandinista handling of the economy was summed up in January 1984 by a special presidential commission headed by Henry Kissinger. Nicaragua's economic performance, the Kissinger report said, was the worst of all Central American nations because of the "mismanagement invariably associated with regimes espousing Marxist-Leninist ideology."[2] In essence the administration argued that the Sandinistas sacrificed the well-being of their people to satisfy Marxist dogma; they stole land from the middle classes, thereby breaking their

Top: Despite President Reagan's ban on trade with Nicaragua, dozens of U.S. firms still operate in that country. The Nicaraguan government cites this as evidence that the country still has a mixed economy. Bottom: Nicaraguans waiting on line for cooking gas. The Contra war and the poor economy have caused widespread shortages.

promise to run a mixed economy; and their economic policies failed, causing hunger and shortages which turned the majority of the people against them.

Not so, say the Sandinistas. They maintain that until the White House unleashed the Contras, the economy was growing faster than in any other country in Latin America. They also believe that the middle classes deliberately mismanaged their farms and businesses for political reasons, and that all Nicaragua's economic problems were caused by the war and by a U.S. effort to overthrow the revolution, motivated by fear that Nicaragua's socialist model was working so well it would inspire other revolutions in the region.

There may be a grain of truth in both arguments, but the results of the first three years favor the Sandinistas. According to the United Nations Economic Commission for Latin America (ECLA), between 1979 and 1983—the start of the Contra war—Nicaragua's cumulative economic growth was 22.5 percent. During that period the economies of the other Central American countries shrank by an average of 5.7 percent. In that same period the real standard of living for each Nicaraguan (gross domestic product per capita) increased 7.7 percent, while it deteriorated by an average of 14.7 percent throughout the rest of the region. Meanwhile Nicaragua's inflation rate and the increase in its foreign debt were comparable to those of its neighbors, and Nicaragua promptly met every payment on its foreign debt, which made it almost unique in Latin America.[3] Moreover the Sandinistas were able to achieve these extraordinary results despite an industrial and agricultural base that had been so damaged by the insurrection that the World Bank had warned that "per capita income levels of 1977 will not be attained, in the best of circumstances, until the late 1980's."[4]

Dependency

So what went wrong after 1983? Was it Marxist policies and mismanagement? Certainly the Sandinistas do have an unabashedly Marxist interpretation of Nicaragua's economic problems. They believe the grinding poverty they inherited from Somoza was the product of "dependent capitalism."[5] In very simple terms the dependency theory is as follows: Most of the goods produced by wealthy countries, such as the U.S., are bought by consumers in those countries; for American industry to thrive, ordinary Americans must have enough money to buy American-made goods, so wages and living standards must be maintained. But in poor Third World countries, like Nicaragua, the most important businesses produce raw commodities, such as sugar or cocoa, which are exported to wealthy nations. So Third World businessmen do not depend on purchases by their workers for profits. Quite the opposite; if they can squeeze wages—and save money by not paying workers for health care or pensions—they can make higher profits.

As a result it is in the interests of big businessmen to exploit their workers, making them work harder for less. This encourages the formation of dictatorships, which protect the elite by preventing workers from protesting and demanding better wages. The Sandinistas believe that in Nicaragua, while individual businessmen may have opposed Somoza, they also took the opportunity of his dictatorship to exploit their workers. "The businessmen were true to their class," one Sandinista trade unionist told the author, "they proved that they would always oppose the democratic aspirations of the workers."

One response to dependency might have been to seize all large land-holdings, give them to the peasants, and encourage them to grow their own food, instead of crops for export. The Sandinistas were well aware that most of the landless peasants belonged to families that at one time or another had been evicted from their own small farms. After the Triumph that course was advocated by some left-wingers. It must have been tempting, especially when the Sandinistas looked at the worst victims of dependency, the impoverished *campesinos* who had been driven to the "agricultural frontier."

The Life of a Peasant

The life of such a peasant was abject. "Home" would be a miserable, earth-floored, single-roomed wooden shack with no electricity or water and the bushes for a toilet. The *campesinos* received virtually no education or health care, and more than one out of every ten *campesino* babies died in their first year, usually from the most basic and easily cured of illnesses such as diarrhea. Children who survived were soon obliged to work, sometimes from as early as age six. Work—especially at harvest time—often meant seven days a week of dawn to dusk, back-breaking labor in fields full of poisonous pesticides, beneath a burning sun. "Luxuries"—meaning perhaps sugar or kerosene—often could only be bought with money borrowed at usurious rates, which condemned entire peasant families to a lifetime cycle of debt.[6]

Rejecting the Classic Marxist Approach

Although the FSLN was determined to "progressively reduce the external dependence of the people of Sandino"[7] and committed to giving land to the landless, it was also determined to create well-paid jobs, to develop the economy by industrializing, and to boost spending on health, education, and other social programs. To do that the Sandinistas would need to earn foreign currency to pay for their ambitious projects, which meant continuing to export cash crops. At first they assumed that the Somoza cotton, coffee, sugar, and cattle estates confiscated by the government were so vast that they would provide a reliable source of foreign income and that little attention would have to be paid to private landowners.

They quickly discovered that they only controlled 25 percent of the export production that earned hard cash.[8] They also soon realized that they did not have enough experienced technicians and managers to effectively run what they had. Not only were further expropriations out of the question, but somehow they would need to retain the cooperation of the large landowners, businessmen, and the middle classes. Instead of imposing a rigid, Marxist-style economy, the new government quickly realized it would have to work within a mixed economy.

So one of the first Sandinista policies was to discourage land seizures by the peasants and large wage claims by the workers. Their heavy spending on health care and education programs helped take the steam out of early wage demands. Private producers were offered guaranteed prices and guaranteed profits for their crops, and bank credits to buy seed, fertilizer, and pesticides. Between 1980 and 1982, for example, 54 percent of the credit extended by the government went to the private sector at minimal interest rates. Meanwhile taxes on exporters were kept deliberately low.[9] More importantly, for the first two years of the revolution there was no agrarian reform program to systematically expropriate land for the landless, whose hopes had been so raised by the Triumph. Left-wing critics lambasted the Sandinistas for being too conservative.

Did the Private Landowners Waste an Opportunity?

Despite these efforts to win support from the large landowners, as early as 1981 a Sandinista official declared, "The private farmers . . . have wasted an historic opportunity."[10] Since then the Sandinistas and the private sector have fought almost constantly, and the economy has suffered. Part of the reason the relationship broke down was political. As we have seen, landowners and businessmen complained, through their organization COSEP, about the political direction the FSLN was taking. Another major problem was insecurity. Despite promises from the Sandinistas to respect private property, factories and farms were seized by peasants and workers, and the government made no attempt to eject them. Indeed, when the courts started to move to return the lands that had been illegally seized after the Triumph, the

Sandinistas responded in March 1980 with a decree legalizing the occupations.

In an effort to restore confidence, in 1981 the government declared that it "guarantees the rights to private property over the land to all those who employ it productively and efficiently." The promise has been frequently repeated. But periodically land has been confiscated for what the owners believe is punishment of political opposition or as a "warning" to the Burgeses to avoid confrontations. For example in 1985 a farm belonging to Enrique Bolaños, then leader of COSEP, was seized, and in 1988 the sugar estates of the millionaire Pellas family were expropriated shortly after a violent anti-government demonstration. To those landowners truly worried about the security of their farms, it clearly made little sense to invest money, time, and energy in maintaining their property.

Another motive for lack of cooperation was the nationalization of the banks and the government control of import and export sales. Previously, when farmers dealt directly with buyers in the United States, they could inflate their purchase invoices for seed and fertilizer and understate their export profits. As a result they were able to stash dollars in American banks. It was to halt precisely such activities in El Salvador that the Reagan administration advised the government there to nationalize the banks and foreign trade.[11] But according to Ramiro Gurdian, the present head of COSEP, the result is that "we only own the property in name, in fact we are managers for the government: they tell us how much profit we can make, they tell us how much we must pay our workers, they tell us how much credit we will get, which determines how much seed we can buy and how much land we can cultivate. This is not free enterprise."[12]

Beyond the psychological disincentive, one practical drawback to this level of government control has been excessive delays caused by bureaucracy, which has interfered with planting and harvesting schedules. For example, government approval is needed to release the dollar reserves needed for foreign purchases of pesticides. When bureaucracy delays these purchases, spraying occurs late, and part of the harvest is lost to insects or disease. In some years the government has been slow to announce what prices it would pay for the crops. The private farmers, unsure if they would be guaranteed a profit, delayed planting, which again reduced the size of the harvest.

To all of these explanations the Sandinistas claim yet another motive for the agricultural problems. They say private landowners refused to cultivate in a deliberate effort to bankrupt the economy and to destabilize the government. Whatever the ultimate reason, the effect was indisputable. In 1981 the government calculated that 30 percent of farmland was idle. Peasant unions produced dozens of examples of farms where owners were selling equipment, driving cattle across the border, pocketing government loans, and allowing fields and coffee plants to deteriorate.[13] As late as 1982 capital flight was still estimated at more than $100 million a year.[14]

Agrarian Reform

In July 1981, after two years of unsatisfactory results from working with private landowners, the Sandinistas announced their agrarian reform program. It was not designed to absorb more land into the state sector, but to satisfy the landless peasants. The opposition had suggested splitting up Somoza's estates for the landless. The idea was considered and quickly rejected; the estates were modern and mechanized, unsuitable for dividing into small peasant plots, and they produced urgently needed cash crops. Instead they became state farms, a term that smacks of the inefficiencies of the Soviet Union, although many have been extremely productive.

The agrarian reform, as it was conceived, only affected the largest farms—those over 864 acres—and then only those abandoned or underutilized. There was also compensation to the owners and an appeals process. In practice,

*A cooperative farm. Cooperatives
have been targets of Contra attacks.*

according to COSEP, the Sandinistas have confiscated smaller farms and farms working at full production. This claim is denied by the government.

In distributing the land, which has so far benefited about 40,000 families, the Sandinistas encouraged the creation of cooperatives for greater efficiency—which was again attacked as "socialist manipulation" by the opposition—but more than 20 percent went to individuals. In the end about a fifth of all farms in the country were expropriated. COSEP complains that the peasants were not given outright ownership, but merely "title" to the land: a farm can be inherited or given to family members, but it cannot be rented or sold without government permission. Opponents suggest this is evidence that the government will eventually take back the land for state farms. The Sandinistas vigorously deny that. They say the restrictions are to prevent the creation of a new class of large landowners.

Titles have also been given to the squatters who moved onto virgin land on the "agricultural frontier," and to Miskitos on their traditional lands on the Caribbean coast. Altogether, by 1987, title to more than 1.2 million acres had been given to peasant families and cooperatives. The government target is that ultimately 40 to 50 percent of farms should be privately owned, 30 to 40 percent should be owned by cooperatives, and 20 percent by the state.[15] In the last few years the pace of land expropriations has slowed, the government has stimulated private landowners with higher profits and even by paying for crops and cattle in dollars, and relations have somewhat improved, though tensions remain.

Industry

But in the industrial sector the problems have been even more acute than on the land. The first problem affecting manufacturing industry predated the Triumph: the largest market for Nicaraguan manufactured goods had been the Central American Common Market, but in the late seventies the Common Market collapsed, leading to lost sales. Industry relied on imported raw materials such as chemicals, iron, steel, glass, leather, paper, and rubber, which had to be paid in increasingly scarce hard cash. In any case, after the Triumph businessmen were unwilling to take advantage of low-interest foreign loans. As the World Bank noted, "The recovery of industrial production has been hampered by the reluctance of the private sector to expand production and to invest." The World Bank blamed lack of government guarantees and the failure of the Sandinistas to establish "clear and consistent rules of the game," which the FSLN believes meant political concessions. As the World Bank predicted, "Given its predominant participation in the productive process, the private sector will largely determine the pace and extent of economic recovery through its investment decisions."[16] Even today Nicaragua continues to be a market-driven economy in which the private sector owns 60 percent of productive capacity and can play a decisive role in the economy.

In late 1981 the government tried to push the private manufacturing sector into doing its share of economic reconstruction. Three well-known businessmen were indicted and sentenced to jail for what amounted to economic sabotage. The effect was the opposite of that intended and merely led to more friction and less investment. Next the government offered industrialists higher profits, but that only led to more capital flight. As foreign exchange became harder to obtain, production lines slowed. The factories were not nationalized; as throughout Central America they simply closed their gates. For many private manufacturers the final straw was to be the U.S. trade embargo, as we shall see.

Surprisingly, despite the tensions with the private sector, production in agriculture and manufacturing is still higher than in 1980. So what explains the terrible shortages that plague the country? There are five major factors: growing demand; the worsening of the "terms of trade"; the U.S.-

inspired aid cut-off and trade embargo; the decimation caused by the Contras; and Sandinista inefficiency.

Growing Demand

Although the Sandinistas tried to hold down wages and convince workers of the need for austerity, their encouragement of trade unions and their reticence in using force to repress strikes in the early years inevitably led to higher spending power. In the countryside, where the Sandinistas provided four times more credit to small farmers than before the Triumph, *campesinos* also found themselves with far more to spend. On top of that the population has been growing extremely rapidly. As a result, demand for food in the first eighteen months of the revolution grew 45 percent. For example, by 1982 people were eating twice as much chicken as in 1977, and pork and rice consumption went up 60 percent. These consumption patterns created huge strains. Even when the Contra war and other factors started to cause production losses, eating habits remained the same, aggravating the effect of the shortages.[17]

Worsening Terms of Trade

Starting in the late 1970s, the prices paid on the international market for most agricultural commodities started to plummet. Sugar is probably the best example. Sugar prices today are still less than half what they were in 1975. Between 1981 and 1983 the prices paid for Nicaragua's exports fell 11.9 percent. At the same time the price of imports rose by exactly the same amount: 11.9 percent. So although production grew 11.2 percent in that period, by 1983 Nicaragua's exports only bought about 80 percent of what they had bought in 1980. This shift in Nicaragua's terms of trade was even worse than in the rest of Central America, but throughout the region low commodity prices have caused the economies of all five republics to contract for seven years in a row.[18]

The U.S. Foreign Aid Cut-off

The World Bank had noted in 1981 that Nicaragua needed foreign loans to build up its export capacity and to restore the economy. If funds were blocked, it would lead to "financial trauma." Yet that is exactly what the Reagan administration did. Between February and April 1981 the White House terminated a total of $118 million in aid, despite intelligence reports indicating that Managua had halted backing for the Salvadoran guerrillas. At the same time U.S. representatives at multilateral lending institutions, such as the World Bank and the Inter-American Development Bank, were ordered to block all loans to Nicaragua. In 1982 Thomas Enders, who was then assistant secretary of state for inter-American affairs, warned that Nicaragua would not be readmitted to the "aid community" until the Sandinistas complied with a series of U.S. demands.[19] The shortage of foreign exchange has not only stopped new projects, it has prevented the government from buying badly needed raw materials, and as we have seen, factories have had to close.

In 1983 the White House unilaterally cut Nicaragua's quota of sugar exports to the U.S. by 90 percent. The move was condemned by the General Agreement on Trade and Tariffs, the international body that regulates world trade, but the measure was not reversed. Ironically, among the worst affected were private landowners, who at the time controlled more than half of the country's sugar production.

The administration used several other tactics to disrupt trade between the two countries, which rapidly escalated in significance. In September and October 1983, CIA-organized teams attacked and destroyed oil storage facilities at the Pacific harbors of Corinto and Puerto Sandino. In January the same teams laid mines in Corinto, Puerto Sandino, and the Caribbean port of El Bluff. The mining provoked an outcry from America's strongest allies, but the protests came too late to prevent the economic repercussions: several fishing boats were sunk, merchant ships were damaged, and delivery of vital imports was delayed.

The Trade Embargo

The biggest blow to trade came on May 1, 1985, when President Reagan certified to Congress that the Nicaraguan government constituted an "unusual and extraordinary threat" to the United States. By executive order he declared a national emergency, and using emergency powers, he imposed an embargo that prohibited all trade between Nicaragua and the U.S. The national emergency is still in effect, as is the embargo. The Sandinistas had anticipated a trade cut-off and managed to find alternative markets for many of their exports, mainly in Western Europe, Canada, and Japan. But imports were a different matter. Nicaraguan factories are largely equipped with American-made machinery and it has proved very difficult to find spare parts elsewhere. It also forced Nicaragua to turn to the Soviet bloc for its imports. In 1984 Eastern Europe accounted for just 15.4 percent of Nicaragua's trade, in 1985 it jumped to 28.8 percent.[20]

The effect of the loss of American and multilateral aid was partly offset by bilateral loans from Western Europe and Latin America, but together with the trade disruption it led to fewer purchases of fertilizers and seeds, spare parts for tractors, harvesters, crop dusting planes, and other agricultural and industrial machinery. This caused production losses, fewer exports, and less cash for imports. It was the start of a vicious spiral.

The Cost of the War

But most damaging of all has been the effect of the war and the cost of Contra attacks. By the end of 1987 the war had caused losses worth $1.15 billion, four times the value of

A village after a Contra attack—the government estimates the Contra war damage at $1.15 billion.

Nicaragua's total exports in 1987.[21] Of that, $171 million was the result of physical destruction: rural schools and clinics, cooperatives, bridges, roads, electricity pylons, grain silos and oil storage tanks, fishing boats, coffee processing equipment, saw mills, trucks, and so on. The effect of this destruction has been felt everywhere: harvests could not be collected, goods could not be delivered to markets and ports, fisherman could not go to sea.

Production losses have amounted to $978 million. But there have been other costs. In 1987 41 percent of the national budget went on defense. Millions have had to be spent on rehousing peasants who have fled, or been forcibly relocated, from their farms in the war zones. Since the peasants are the major producers of essential foodstuffs, their production has had to be replaced with expensive irrigation projects on the Pacific coast or with even more expensive imports. Those refugees who have moved to Managua have placed an intolerable load on services (one of the contributing factors to the water shortages in the capital). Skilled workers have been mobilized from their jobs in factories and farms to fight in the army, causing yet more production losses. The war has forced the government to redirect consumer goods such as clothing to the army. For example, half the country's shoe production is now dedicated to making boots for the army. This contributes directly to the shortages and lines in Managua.

Sandinista Mismanagement

Compounding all these problems has been the Sandinista youth and inexperience, which led to spendthrift social programs, inefficiency, and an overly bureaucratic intervention in the marketplace. For example, in an effort to let everyone taste the fruits of the Triumph, in 1979 the Sandinistas started to subsidize all basic foodstuffs. Until at least 1984 food prices were considerably lower in Nicaragua than anywhere else in Central America. Corn became so cheap that many coffee and cotton farmers who had once grown corn for their workers stopped doing so because it was cheaper to buy it from the government. Corn production consequently plummeted. In an effort to ensure that everyone received a minimum supply each week of rice, beans, and other staples, the Sandinistas made farmers repay their loans with a portion of their crops, but the government distribution service was terribly inefficient.

Another problem was the budget deficit. Ever since the Triumph, the government has been living beyond its means. The food subsidies knocked a big hole in government spending. Since 1979 more than 20 percent of the budget has gone to social services—health, education, and housing—which do not provide any direct financial return.[22] Many farmers could not get their crops to market, or their crops rotted because of poor storage, so they defaulted on their loans. This also boosted the deficit. State farms invested a good portion of their profits building schools and health clinics, instead of contributing the funds to help balance the budget. Once the war started, the government had to spend huge sums on weapons and clothing and food for the troops. All this meant that the government spent far more than it received. To cover the gap, the Central Bank simply printed more money. The result was inflation, then by 1987 hyper-inflation, and terrible scarcities.

TEN

HOLY WAR

In the first week of December each year, Nicaragua grinds to a halt. Factories close, markets are deserted, families head for the beach, men get drunk on rum and beer. It is the Festival of La Purisima, dedicated to the Virgin Mary, the high point of the nation's religious calendar. About 85 percent of Nicaraguans consider themselves devout Roman Catholics and the tradition of Purisima runs deep. The FSLN has made no attempt to interfere. Quite the opposite, each year during the festival government workers build a half dozen altars in the streets, and on the evening of December 7th you will find Sandinista *comandantes* and the Marxist president himself standing beside these shrines to the Virgin, doling out candy and gifts to little children. Above their heads flutter banners proclaiming *Entre Cristianismo y Revolución no Hay Contradicción!* (Between Christianity and revolution there is no contradiction!). But isn't there? And if not, why did President Reagan accuse the Sandinistas of crushing religion?

On the one hand Sandinista respect for religion seems overwhelming. Four Catholic priests have been or continue

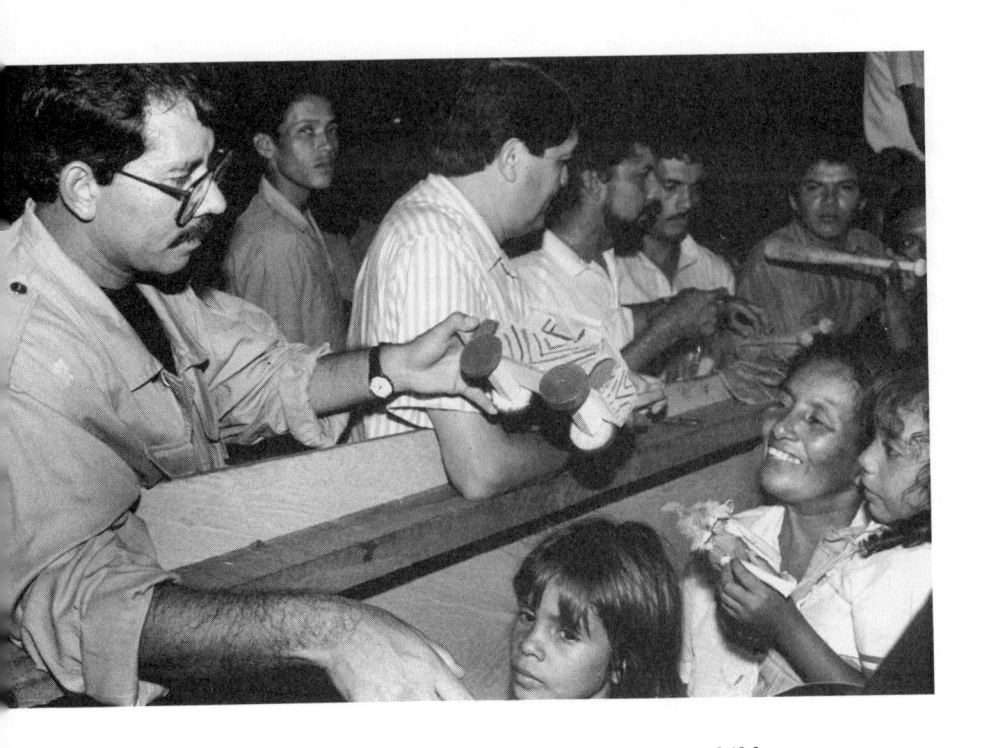

Daniel Ortega distributing toys to children at a celebration of the feast of La Purisima, Nicaragua's most important religious holiday.

to be members of Nicaragua's revolutionary government: Edgardo Parrales as minister of social welfare; Ernesto Cardenal as minister of culture; Fernando Cardenal as minister of education; and Miguel D'Escoto as foreign minister. Another priest, Gaspar Garcia Laviana, fought with the Sandinistas, was promoted to comandante, and was killed by the Guardia in 1978. His portrait, together with those of other Sandinista "martyrs" and more conventional saints, is part of a mural that decorates a church in the poor Managua barrio of Riguero. Shortly after the Triumph the San-

Ernesto Cardenal: "guerrilla poet," Sandinista Minister of Culture, and Roman Catholic priest.

dinistas issued a communique praising the role Catholics had played in the insurrection, particularly Archbishop Miguel Obando y Bravo, and acknowledging that many people had joined the revolution out of religious conviction. In July 1979, when the archbishop led a series of religious services to celebrate the Triumph, the idea of religious persecution seemed ridiculous.

But on the other hand, the Sandinistas have arrested several priests and accused them of counter-revolutionary activity. Fifteen foreign priests, one Nicaraguan monsignor, and a bishop have all been expelled from the country or barred reentry. The police have confiscated a Church newsletter printing plant and twice shut down Radio Catolica, the Catholic radio station. Sandinista mobs have frequently jeered and jostled the bishops. And when Pope John Paul II visited Nicaragua in March 1983, Sandinista supporters angrily shouted him down. There is obviously a conflict between the two extremes, but it has more to do with a fight within the Church than a battle between Marxism and Christianity.

Religious History

The roots of the conflict go back to the Second Vatican Council (1962–65), known popularly as "Vatican II," when Roman Catholic leaders attempted to revitalize their Church and make it more accessible. Among other measures, they decided that services should be conducted in the vernacular instead of Latin and that lay participation should be increased. Vatican II inspired the conference of Latin American bishops at Medellín in 1968, which called on priests to "defend the rights of the oppressed." In what became known as the "Preferential Option for the Poor," priests throughout Latin America were galvanized into action to improve the living conditions for peasants and slum dwellers. The effort politicized them.

In Nicaragua the Church became increasingly critical

of the dictatorship. In 1968 seven priests wrote to Somoza urging him to stop torturing and killing opponents. He labeled them "the Marxist priests."[1] In the aftermath of the 1972 earthquake priests were elbowed out of relief operations, only to witness grotesque corruption in the midst of the tragedy. In 1972 and 1974 Archbishop Obando refused to bless the inauguration of either the triumvirate or the third presidency of Anastasio Somoza Debayle.

In 1974 Obando also mediated between Somoza and the FSLN commando unit which had seized hostages at Chema Castillo's Christmas party. He repeated the role in 1978 when the FSLN seized the National Palace. Both operations were extremely popular in Nicaragua because they humiliated Somoza; rightly or wrongly Obando was associated with their success, and it was assumed that he sympathized with the Sandinistas' radical demands. This reaction increased the Church's prestige and encouraged people to oppose the dictatorship.

The Church's growing political involvement continued. In 1977 the bishops issued a pastoral letter accusing the Guardia of killing more than 200 peasants. In August 1978 the bishops called on Somoza to resign, and just before the Triumph they announced that the people had a right to rebel. Finally in November 1979 the bishops went so far as to give lukewarm support to socialism: "if Socialism means . . . a genuine transfer of power toward the popular classes, it will find nothing in the Christian faith but motivation and support."[2]

While this was happening, the Church had tried to compensate for a severe shortage of priests by training lay preachers called Delegates of the Word. These preachers were often peasants and workers; to them the Preferential Option for the Poor was even more inspirational than it was to the priests. The delegates fanned out through cities and mountain communities and founded bible study groups called Ecclesiastical Base Communities (CEBs) where the faithful tried to apply Christ's message to everyday life.

They came to see Jesus as a "proletarian revolutionary" who had fought injustice in this world instead of just waiting for heaven in the next, and to regard the misery in their lives as a sin perpetrated by an evil government against which it was right to fight.[3] God became *el Dios de los Pobres*, the God of the Poor. In other countries this interpretation of the Gospel became known as Liberation Theology, in Nicaragua it was called La Iglesia Popular, the Popular Church, as distinct from the Traditional Church.

Liberation Theology has had a profound influence throughout Latin America, especially in poor communities where the fatalistic acceptance of poverty and deprivation has been replaced by social and political militancy. In Central America in particular, the combination of devout faith and the ardor of passions provoked by injustice has supplied recruits and strength to revolutionary movements. It has even affected the Communist regime in Cuba, where President Fidel Castro has become far more tolerant of the Catholic Church because he now believes it may be a sort of ally in the struggle for social justice and a more egalitarian society.

In Nicaragua during the 1970s many Christians became politically active and started to support the Sandinistas. So the CEBs became targets of the Guardia. Delegates of the Word and their converts were shot, tortured, and raped, which simply radicalized the priesthood even more. Several priests started to hide fugitive Sandinista leaders and to give them help. Ernesto Cardenal, who had founded a religious peasant community in the sixties, encouraged his followers to join the FSLN. They saw it as an extension of their Christian faith, and in 1977 they attacked a Guardia barracks. It was, they said, "a violence of love."[4] Another priest, Uriel Molina, led a bible-study class in Managua which attracted several university students from rich families. The students were so affected that they too joined the FSLN—one of them, Luis Carrion, rose to become a member of the Sandinista National Directorate.

Two Sorts of Faith

As a result many Sandinistas came to associate aspects of Christianity with Marxism and nationalism, a "synthesis of Christian vocation and revolutionary conscience," the FSLN called it.[5] As early as 1969 Carlos Fonseca had drawn parallels between Christianity and Sandinism.[6] Indeed the Sandinistas' belief in their cause is almost messianic: those who die in combat are called martyrs; Sandinistas address each other as "brother" or "sister"; Interior Minister Tomas Borge, a Marxist hard-liner, has decorated his office with crucifixes and often talks about creating an "earthly paradise" while other Sandinistas even refer to the "Kingdom of God." In 1985 when Daniel Ortega named Fernando Cardenal minister of education, he ended his speech shouting *"Pueblo de Sandino, pueblo de Cristo!"* (Land of Sandino, land of Christ!).

Encouraged by this official embrace of Liberation Theology, thousands of foreign priests, nuns, religious workers, and progressive Catholics poured into Nicaragua. Here at last, they thought, was a government that would help them to carry out their Preferential Option for the Poor. Nicaragua became a crucible in which to test revolutionary Catholicism. The CEBs continued with their democratic reinterpretation of the Gospel, and together with the new arrivals, they enthusiastically backed the Marxist government. The Sandinistas for their part decided to "neutralize wherever possible the influence of conservative pastors and to have closer ties with priests sympathetic to the revolution."[7]

Obando Becomes an Opponent

To the Catholic hierarchy all this was profoundly disturbing, much more so than any mere attempt to repress the Church. It undermined their authority and threatened to subvert

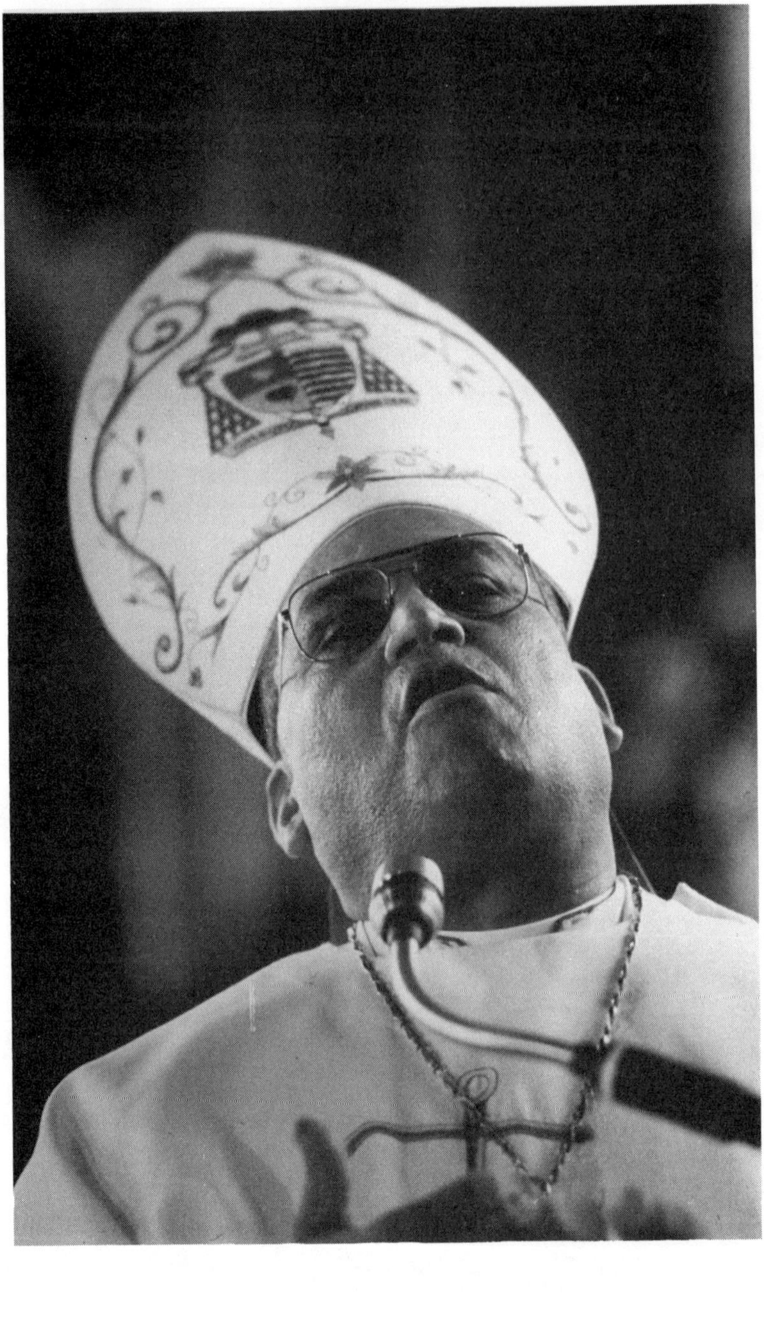

their religion. They saw it as "a species of fifth column, or a column within the Church that is at the same time an enemy of the Church."[8] This fear led Obando to take an increasingly prominent anti-Sandinista role. Despite his early mediation efforts between the Sandinistas and Somoza and his tentative recognition of the Sandinista government in 1979, this was not a profound switch for the archbishop.

Obando is from a humble background and has little reputation as an intellectual or theologian. He made his name through hard work in visiting far-flung mountainous parishes. Like the *campesinos* his natural political instincts have always been conservative and he was deeply suspicious of the Sandinistas even before they came to power. He was a member of the conservative delegation that flew to Caracas in July 1979 in a last-ditch attempt to prevent a Sandinista victory. Although immediately after the Triumph he went along with the other bishops in accepting the FSLN, he soon set up "leadership-training workshops" to develop anti-Sandinista activists, and he became increasingly virulent in his opposition as the years went by.

The first major trial of strength between Obando and the Sandinistas came in May 1980, when the council of bishops ordered the priests in the government to quit their jobs. The order was ignored. When the bishops tried to remove pro-Sandinista parish priests, the churches were occupied by angry parishioners who thought they had a right to demand a priest of their liking, and when the bishops appeared on the streets or at the occupied churches,

Cardinal Miguel Obando y Bravo, leader of the Roman Catholic Church in Nicaragua, has clashed frequently with the Sandinistas over the political direction of the revolution.

they were harassed by *turbas* in an effort to get them to accept the "popular will."

The Magisterium

But Catholicism is not a democratic faith; the Pope is the successor of Saint Peter and in matters of doctrine and morality he is officially "infallible"; his word is law. Just nine months before the Triumph a new Pope had been elected, Karol Wojtyla of Poland, John Paul II, whose whole life had been spent confronting a Marxist government and whose major concern was that Vatican II had got out of hand and undermined the authority of the Papal See. He was determined to change that and to restore the Magisterium, the teaching authority of Rome.9 To him Nicaragua must have looked like the perfect test case, and he automatically sympathized with Obando. His bishops had to be obeyed.

In March 1983 John Paul II visited Nicaragua. Before a crowd that might have numbered as many as 750,000 people he delivered a stern lecture. The Iglesia Popular, he said, is "an absurd and dangerous object." He condemned "unacceptable ideological commitments, temporal options, or concepts of the church which are contrary to the true one." He repeatedly demanded obedience to the bishops. Sandinistas who had hoped to hear a condemnation of the Contras—who by then had already caused several hundred deaths including those of seventeen teenagers just three days before the Pope arrived—started to chant "we want peace" and "popular power." The Pope shouted *"silencio,"* they ignored him. Then as he said Mass a government-sponsored group called the Mothers of the Heroes and Martyrs crowded on stage begging for a prayer for their dead sons. To the Pope it must have represented everything he most feared and disliked about the Popular Church: the fusing of the Christian concept of martyrs with veneration for dead Marxist troops. He refused. The Mass ended in pandemonium.

The Cardinal Attacks

As far as many Catholics were concerned, the Sandinistas had disgraced themselves and Obando had been given the Pope's personal support. For the next two years Obando exploited this moral boost. At the end of 1983 the government introduced conscription, in order to face the growing CIA-funded Contra army. Obando responded with a pastoral letter which challenged the Sandinistas' authority and encouraged youths to break the law by refusing to obey the draft. He said "absolute dictatorship of a political party which is constituted by force . . . poses the problem of legitimacy as well as the legitimacy of its institutions including the army . . . the attitude toward this bill for all those who do not share the Sandinista Party ideology has to be that of conscientious objection."[10] Priests started to hide draft dodgers under the pretext that they were seminarians.

In April 1985 Obando was elevated to cardinal, and on his return from Rome he stopped in Miami, where he said Mass at a service attended by top Contra leaders. "I do not object to being identified with the people who have taken up arms," he told journalists.[11] His words encouraged the Contras. They printed leaflets and posters proclaiming "Cardinal Obando is with us!" and started to recruit support in the mountains by telling peasants that the Sandinistas would prevent them from practicing their religion. Indeed since 1983 the CIA had been teaching the Contras to use Christian slogans in a psychological-warfare training manual. And according to Edgar Chamorro, a former Contra leader, the CIA set up an organization called the Puebla Institute to exploit the religious issue.[12]

As far as the government was concerned, Obando had allied himself with President Reagan's efforts to overthrow the revolution. Obando insisted on negotiations between the Sandinistas and the Contras; he condemned Sandinista human rights abuses but disclaimed any knowledge of Contra atrocities and refused to condemn them. In 1985, at his insistence, the Vatican unfrocked the education minister, Fernando Cardenal. At a press conference Cardenal tearfully insisted that "to abandon the revolution would be a grave sin." In 1985 President Reagan described Obando as "a great hero of truth and courage" and claimed that the cardinal had been "prevented from speaking freely to his flock,"[13] which was not quite true—Obando had been told he could not conduct open-air services. The conflict degenerated to the point where in 1986 the president was able to quote Obando's deputy, Bishop Pablo Antonio Vega, in support of his appeal for $100 million for the Contras.

The Sandinistas also pointed out that at the start of the Reagan administration Republican ideologues had recommended a campaign against Liberation Theology. That recommendation was followed up by a major political and fund-raising campaign by right-wing American religious organizations. The Sandinistas believed that the funds Obando received from a variety of U.S. sources were evidence of his complicity with the CIA.[14] His sermons became regular and thinly veiled attacks on the FSLN, and he removed at least thirty pro-Sandinista priests and nuns from their jobs. As several businessmen admitted, Obando's outspoken stance transformed him from a spiritual leader into the symbolic leader of the political opposition to the Sandinistas.[15]

It was in that context that the government censored Obando's pastoral letters, closed down Radio Catolica, sent their mobs to demonstrate against him, arrested his priests, and tried to restrict his movements. And it was these activities that led the cardinal to complain of "persecution" of the church, a cry which President Reagan happily took up.

There can be no doubt that the Sandinistas have tried to use the Catholic Church to their advantage by encouraging the members of the Iglesia Popular, just as there can be no doubt that Obando and his supporters in the Church have tried to help destabilize the government; indeed in 1985 Obando's politics led to open divisions between the bishops.

But the FSLN has not indulged in the sort of persecution seen in El Salvador or Guatemala, where priests have been murdered or "disappeared," and the Sandinistas have shown great trust in the Church by putting Jesuits in charge of educating the next generation of Nicaraguans (for example, the minister of education is a Jesuit). The government has continued to negotiate with Catholic leaders, tensions between the two sides have abated since the worst moments in 1983, and in 1988 the Sandinistas invited Obando to mediate negotiations between the government and the Contras. He accepted.

ELEVEN

FROM REAGAN TO BUSH

If, as many argue, the Sandinistas represent a new chapter in revolutionary socialism for their tolerance of religion, political opposition, and private business, that tolerance only appears to last as long as those forces stay within the framework of the ultimate march to an as-yet not clearly defined brand of Sandinista socialism. In the meantime their readiness to clamp down on Church leaders, businessmen, and political opponents who sympathize with U.S. policy or the Contras gave the Reagan administration the ammunition it needed to win congressional support for its Contra policy.

The Sandinistas remain convinced that the Reagan administration's talk of human rights, the Church, and the economy was a smoke screen to hide the real goal: the complete overthrow of their government. But in 1983 they decided to prove that they had a genuine commitment to pluralism and democracy. They announced elections for 1985, which were subsequently brought forward to November 1984.

Sandinista Democracy

Elections were not a concept that the Sandinistas were particularly fond of. As Humberto Ortega had lectured the literacy volunteers in 1980, "Democracy is not simply elections. It is something more, much more. For a revolutionary, for a Sandinista, it means participation by the people in political, economic, social, and cultural affairs. The more people participate in such matters, the more democratic they will be."[1] Another member of the DN, Bayardo Arce, told a meeting of the Socialist Party in 1984 that elections were "bourgeois details" and "bothersome," and he suggested it was time to consider "eliminating all this, let's call it, façade of pluralism."[2]

The Sandinistas make a distinction between "bourgeois" and "popular" democracy. They say that bourgeois democracy—such as in the U.S.—is an illusion. People are allowed to feel that they have political power because once every four years they can elect a new government, but "elections have never changed which class holds power," says Tomas Borge. He believes the outcome of U.S. elections is determined by the media, which are part of a self-perpetuating, wealthy capitalist elite and, he says, that is why half of all Americans don't bother to vote.[3] Popular democracy, according to the Comandantes, occurs when everyone regularly participates in organizations like trade unions or the Sandinista Defense Committees and influences policy decisions. But, as even left-wing critics have complained, popular democracy and elections are not mutually exclusive. Who, for example, is to choose the leader of the unions if there is no vote? And if union leaders are not elected, how will they be responsive to their members' wishes? In Nicaragua, especially in the early years of the revolution, the Sandinistas tended to nominate leaders from above, to impose policies from above, and to merely seek a show of hands as a rubber stamp of approval.[4]

Yet the Sandinistas insist they are truly democratic, because the FSLN itself is a vehicle for the concerns and demands of ordinary citizens and because the raison d'être of the government is to serve the exploited, not the exploiters. From the early days of the revolution, the entire Junta would regularly visit poor neighborhoods to attend televised public meetings called "Face the People." The people were encouraged to vent their frustration bluntly and vociferously. Cabinet ministers were obliged to attend, and this meant that, for example, if someone complained about food shortages (as they usually did), Daniel Ortega could say "here is the minister of commerce, he will answer." That, the Sandinistas argued, is true democracy.

The electoral events of November 1984 were thus not for domestic consumption. They were scripted for a different agenda, the need to convince international opinion, especially in the United States and Western Europe, that the FSLN was not repressive and that it did respect pluralism. If that could be done, they hoped, the Contra war might recede, or at least the government would continue to receive European financial backing.

Elections

There were two problems facing the Sandinistas. First, it was by no means certain that the FSLN still commanded majority support, as most experts agreed they had done in the first three years of the revolution. Secondly, the Reagan administration was bitterly divided over its response. While diplomats argued that the elections offered a genuine opportunity to expand opposition influence in Nicaragua and might even force the FSLN to govern by coalition, the hard-liners said elections would merely "legitimize Communist rule."[5] The ideologues saw the elections as an opportunity to discredit the Sandinistas by organizing a boycott, based on the predetermined conclusion that the elections would be fraudulent. If they were successful, maybe they could persuade Congress to resume aid to the Contras. The president's position was soon apparent; on July 19th, before the Junta had even announced the election rules and before any campaigning had begun, President Reagan dismissed the election as a "Soviet-style sham."[6]

In 1982 three small opposition parties, two trade unions, and COSEP had formed a center-right alliance called the Coordinadora Democrática Nicaragüense (CDN), the Nicaraguan Democratic Coordinator. Linked to the Coordinadora was one wing of the divided Conservative Party. In a typical display of opposition factionalism, the Conservatives refused to formally join the CDN because "our party is so large that we do not need to form alliances," one leader told the author. Within months the two Conservative parties would both divide again to create four parties.

If the opposition was slow to go to work in 1979 and 1980, by 1984 it had become virtually moribund. The parties in the Coordinadora rarely held rallies, even though indoor meetings were permitted. They made little attempt to recruit new members (the Conservatives—supposedly the largest opposition party—did not even possess a list of members in 1984). They squabbled constantly among themselves over tactics, and they did not even have a political platform.

In El Salvador, under conditions of much worse repression, the opposition organized strikes and demonstrations, produced illegal pamphlets, and galvanized support. In Nicaragua the ten legal opposition political parties had offices around the country, phones, legal newsletters, vehicles, and freedom to travel. They even had giant advertising billboards around Managua carrying messages such as "Conservatism Is Free Trade Unions." The apathy was caused by their biggest weakness: they did not have a single leader of stature. Publicly this meant they were overshadowed by Cardinal Obando, and privately it left them dominated by the most right-wing elements of COSEP. Recognizing this weakness in their own ranks, in July 1984 the leaders of the Coordinadora invited Arturo Cruz to be their presidential candidate.

Cruz is a dry-as-dust banker and a lackluster campaigner. But he was untainted by the Somoza era, he had

Arturo Cruz, a former Sandinista high official, briefly ran as an opposition candidate for president in 1984 and subsequently became a leader of the Contras.

worked diligently for the Sandinistas, and when he abandoned them he did not join the Contras. He had all the characteristics the CDN members liked to see in themselves—reasonable, moral, a Western-style democrat. But he had one major failing: he was not a politician, and that flaw would cost the opposition dearly. Also, at the time of his candidacy he was being paid by the CIA. Nevertheless, under pressure from the State Department, Cruz accepted the nomination.[7] But even before he arrived in Nicaragua, the COSEP hard-liners had decided to pull out of the elections, "Don't worry, we're not really going to participate," Mario Rappaccioli, a Conservative leader, told the author at the press conference announcing Cruz's candidacy, "we'll demonstrate the elections are a farce and withdraw."[8]

In July the Coordinadora was finally able to agree on a minimum program, summarized in nine points, almost all of which were political ultimatums rather than demands for electoral guarantees. The last point was the most controversial: that the FSLN negotiate with the Contras. One Latin American diplomat described the nine points as "a challenge to the government to declare political bankruptcy and call in the international receivers." They were announced as "preconditions" for CDN participation in the elections. The day after Cruz returned, he announced that the ninth point was now essential. He would not register as a presidential candidate unless the Sandinistas allowed Contra leaders to stand in the elections. "Many are my friends," he explained, "I could not participate, knowing they could not." European diplomats thought Cruz's demand should have been the centerpiece of a campaign platform. "As an excuse for pulling out it won't do," one said. "It's as if he is deliberately looking for an excuse not to stand." Another thought it signaled that the coordinator was giving up the "political game" and "relying on the Americans to put them in power."[9]

Cruz held three election rallies, all of which led to clashes between Sandinista mobs and CDN followers, but the meetings demonstrated that Cruz could count on some support. Also, in a rare display of openness Sandinista TV broadcast one of Cruz's speeches, in which he venomously attacked the FSLN as the culprit for the war. Yet the deadline for registration came and went without Cruz. Six opposition parties did register, and following negotiations with them, the Sandinistas swiftly moved to lift most of the elements of the state of emergency to allow a freer campaign. Cruz left the country.

But then, prompted by the State Department, the White House team supporting the Contras agreed to drop the most unreasonable points from Cruz's list of demands. From Washington, Cruz was told to change his position, and he informed the FSLN of "his" revised demands. The new list seemed reasonable or at least negotiable. This created the prospect that the Sandinistas might be able to draw the Coordinadora into the campaign and thus end all accusations that the elections were undemocratic, so the FSLN offered to reopen the period for registration of candidates. Then the CIA and U.S. conservatives advised Cruz not to register.[10]

This political *samba* ended in Río de Janeiro on the weekend of September 30th, when Cruz negotiated for two days with Bayardo Arce of the DN, in the shadow of the final registration deadline of October 1st. Arce agreed to postpone the election and gave Cruz guarantees that the voting would be fair. Cruz phoned the CDN leaders and told them to register; they refused. Cruz asked Arce for two days to sway his colleagues. Arce claimed that Cruz was not negotiating seriously and that the FSLN was being made to look foolish: he stormed out of the meeting. It was all over. The CDN would not participate in the election.

Was It "Free and Fair?"

On November 4, 1984, the election went ahead with the FSLN opposed on the left by the Trotskyist Popular Action Movement, the Communist Party, and the Socialist Party, and on the right by the Popular Social Christians, the Inde-

A scene from the 1984 elections in which the Sandinistas won 67 percent of the vote. The Reagan administration dismissed the elections as fraudulent.

pendent Liberals, and the Democratic Conservatives. The Sandinistas won 67 percent of the votes and sixty-one seats in the new National Assembly. The opposition parties won 29 percent of the votes and thirty-five seats. When abstentions, blank votes, and opposition ballots are deducted from the total number of registered voters, Sandinista support was actually about half the electorate, which is hardly typical of "Soviet-style elections."

The Sandinistas had undoubtedly enjoyed and sometimes abused the advantages of incumbency and control of the TV, but most observers believed that the result was fair. Lord Chitnis of the British Liberal Party compared the election to the U.S.-backed versions in El Salvador and concluded "There can be no reason whatever why President Elect Ortega cannot be considered to be the democratically elected leader of Nicaragua."[11]

Two days after the Nicaraguan elections Ronald Reagan was reelected in a forty-nine-state landslide. Even as the results were coming in, U.S. intelligence sources leaked reports that Soviet advanced MIG fighter aircraft were about to arrive at the port of Corinto. Pentagon sources spoke about "surgical strikes"; supersonic American spy planes flew over Managua, setting off terrifying sonic booms; more maneuvers were announced in Honduras, and the Sandinistas once again panicked in the belief that, flush with victory, President Reagan might decide to invade. This time the reaction was the opposite of the 1983 concessions. Tanks were sent into the streets of the city to guard power stations and other vital points, the militias mobilized, censorship was tightened, and the state of emergency resumed. It was just what the conservatives wanted.

Back to the War

The aircraft turned out to be not MIGs but rather MI-25 Hind helicopters. Nicknamed the "flying tank," the MI-25s were possibly the best ground-attack helicopters in the world, and they gave the Sandinistas a tremendous advantage against the Contras. The Sandinista army had also been reorganized: seventeen well-trained Irregular Warfare Battalions started to drive the Contras out of the country. In the south a swift operation drove Pastora from the eight base camps he had established inside Nicaragua. The government created free-fire zones near the northern border by evacuating 7,000 peasant families. Among them were many who had given the Contras information, food, and support; their loss was a big blow to the FDN. The combined effect of these measures helped the Sandinistas rout the Contras. By the end of 1985 most of the "freedom fighters" were stuck in their bases inside Honduras. In the White House people began to grope for desperate measures.

For his part President Reagan decided to confront Congress and force it to resume aid to the Contras. His tactic was to make a series of speeches and television appeals in which the rhetorical volume was progressively turned up. Nicaragua became a "totalitarian dungeon"; Daniel Ortega a "tin-pot dictator"; the Contras "freedom fighters ... the moral equivalent of the Founding Fathers." Congressmen who voted against Contra-aid found themselves targeted in TV ads as "soft on Communism." On May 1, 1985, the nation was told Nicaragua represented such a threat that it justified declaring a national emergency to give the president power to ban all trade with Managua.

Nevertheless, the House of Representatives held out and rejected aid in April. But immediately after that vote, Daniel Ortega made a sudden and unexplained visit to Moscow. Sandinista officials and foreign diplomats subsequently told the author and other journalists that Mexico had halted oil shipments, the situation was desperate, and Ortega had to persuade the Russians to help.[12] But in Washington it looked like a snub to Congress. The FDN in the meantime had moved to improve its violent image, under prodding from the White House. A new civilian leadership was created which drew together Cruz, Robelo, and Calero. The Contras renamed themselves the United Nicaraguan Opposition. It seemed to convince a few lawmakers. In June 1985

*The Sandinista Popular Army has become
—with Soviet and Cuban support—
the most powerful military force in Central America.*

Congress reversed itself and granted the Contras $27 million of nonlethal aid, but following the illegal mining of Nicaragua's harbors and the assassination manual, the CIA was barred from distributing the aid.

Further lobbying by the White House led eventually in June 1986 to $100 million for the Contras, including $70 million for weapons. The Sandinistas reacted with their strongest repression yet. *La Prensa* was closed, the Catholic radio station was shut down, a bishop and priest were expelled from the country, and other opposition figures were arrested, issued warnings, or harassed. These were the sort of measures the White House had been hoping for, as they justified an even stronger reaction from the U.S. But soon the whole strategy started to unravel.

The Iran-Contra Affair

On October 5, 1986, Sandinista troops shot down a C-123 cargo plane. One of the crew, a former U.S. Marine called Eugene Hasenfus, bailed out and was captured. Hasenfus said he was part of a CIA operation to deliver weapons to the Contras, an activity prohibited by Congress since October 1984. Documents found in the plane appeared to corroborate Hasenfus's claim and also linked the pilot to Lieutenant Colonel Oliver North, an official who worked at the White House for the National Security Council. Journalists, congressional committees, and the FBI started to investigate. The House Judiciary Committee asked for a special prosecutor to examine the activities of North, CIA Director Casey, and National Security Adviser John Poindexter. On November 3, 1986, a magazine in Lebanon revealed that the White House had sold weapons to Iran. The next day, in mid-term elections, the Democratic Party made a comeback and seized control of the Senate.

On November 25, 1986 Reagan and his Attorney General Edwin Meese held a press conference and revealed to a stunned nation that arms had indeed been sold to Iran in an effort to secure release of American hostages in Beirut, and that profits from the Iranian sales had been used to buy weapons for the Contras.

Congress decided to hold hearings. All the key players in the administration's Nicaragua policy were obliged to testify. The origin of the scandal reached back to October 1984, when aid to the Contras was cut. President Reagan had then told his national security adviser, Robert McFarlane, to keep the Contras together "body and soul." McFarlane had passed the instruction to North who took it as *carte blanche* to ignore Congress and continue supplying the Contras with weapons and intelligence.

North had taken a three-pronged approach. He enlisted the help of retired General John Singlaub, head of the World Anti-Communist League. Together they approached wealthy American patrons and persuaded them to donate funds—often with the inducement of a private meeting with the President. Some of the money went through a conservative fund-raiser, Spitz Channel (who had paid for the TV ads that attacked congressional opponents of Contra aid). In 1987 Channel pleaded guilty to tax fraud and named North as a co-conspirator.

The second prong involved another fiercely anti-Communist ally, retired Air Force Major General Richard Secord. With North's assistance, Secord created a maze of overseas companies and secret bank accounts that was called the "Enterprise." With President Reagan's approval the "Enterprise" sold weapons to the Iranians in an effort to release the hostages in Beirut. What the President apparently did not know was that profits from those sales were used to buy weapons, principally in Portugal but also in the Eastern bloc, using end-user certificates that falsely stated the ultimate destination of the arms. The weapons went to the Contras through a network, created with unauthorized CIA help, in El Salvador and Costa Rica.

The third source of funds was friendly allies around the world. Among those who helped were Saudi Arabia, Taiwan, and Brunei. South Africa and Israel were also approached. One of the key figures in this international soliciting effort was Elliott Abrams, who in July 1985 became assistant secretary of state for inter-American affairs.

"The Enterprise"

To accompany the money-raising and arms-purchasing side of the "Enterprise," North set up a secret communications network and used his own operatives to keep the operation working smoothly. Most of his activities had the knowledge and support of Casey at the CIA and McFarlane's successor as national security adviser, Vice-Admiral John Poindexter. North, Poindexter, and Abrams all admitted lying to Congress about their activities, and when the scandal broke, North tried to cover up what he had done by destroying all the documents. Perhaps the most shocking element of North's testimony was that Casey had allegedly proposed using the "Enterprise" on a permanent basis. The plan was that the "Enterprise" would maintain a permanent fundraising capacity through contacts among friendly governments, conservative financiers, and secret arms sales. These funds would be channeled through a series of secret bank accounts to pay for secret operatives, a secret communications network, secret arms purchases, and a secret arms delivery capability. As a result the "Enterprise" would be able to intervene in internal conflicts anywhere in the world, even if Congress vetoed such covert action.

The congressional Iran-Contra hearings were very damaging to the Contra cause. They revealed that the Contras had artificially inflated their numbers, that they had designed their military strategy not so much to defeat the Sandinistas as to win support in Washington, and that their much vaunted reforms had been cosmetically applied by North. With both the Contras and the anti-Communist zealots exposed, and the Sandinistas anxious to avoid the consequences of $100 million in fresh Contra aid, an opportunity presented itself once more for negotiations. The opportunity was seized by the newly elected president of Costa Rica, Oscar Arias.

The Arias Plan

On August 6, 1987, the presidents of the five Central American countries met in Guatemala to hear a proposal from Arias which had been worked out in advance with the Democratic Speaker of the House of Representatives, Jim Wright. The plan called for an immediate ceasefire throughout the region; a cutoff of aid to all the regional guerrilla movements; an amnesty for all rebels followed by internal dialogue with unarmed political opponents; democratization and free elections; a halt to the use by guerrillas of territory in any regional state to attack another state; and international verification. The plan was accepted.

The news came as a profound shock to Abrams and other hard-liners in Washington. Abrams tried to persuade U.S. allies in Central America to back away from the plan, but they refused. This demonstrated the extent to which the Iran-Contra affair had undermined U.S. authority in the region.[14]

The administration did not stop trying. On September 10, 1987, the White House announced that it would request an astonishing $270 million for the Contras. But on October 13th Arias was awarded the Nobel Peace Prize. Arias and the presidents of El Salvador and Honduras all urged Congress to postpone any aid vote. In the following months the Sandinistas reopened *La Prensa* and the Catholic radio station. They appointed their bitter enemy, Cardinal Obando, to head the reconciliation talks with domestic political opponents. They abolished the Tribunales Populares (the special courts) and allowed opposition demonstrations. In November they accepted indirect talks with the Contras mediated by Obando, and in January 1988 they accepted direct talks.

On February 3, 1988, the House of Representatives rejected Contra aid. A second vote in March produced the same outcome. The Contras were fast running out of funds, which meant they too had a reason to talk. On March 23rd the Contras met the Sandinistas at Sapoa, just inside Nicaragua near the Costa Rican border. They agreed to a ninety-day ceasefire. Again the hard-liners were totally dismayed. By mid-1988, under pressure from Abrams, the Contras had escalated their demands in the negotiations aimed at a comprehensive peace settlement. The Sandinistas reacted by clamping down on their domestic opposition once again. But the ceasefire continued, and the possibility of a negotiated solution remained open as President George Bush moved into the White House.

The Bush Administration

Like the Reagan administration, the Bush administration came into office facing a crisis in Central America. At the beginning of 1989 the guerrillas in El Salvador were promising a major new offensive. Para-military groups had started to respond by stepping up kidnappings and assassinations of civilians. At the same time surveys showed the right-wing Arena party was likely to win the general and presidential elections in March. Arena is led by Roberto d'Aubuisson, who has long been linked to death-squad activity. As this book went to press, a Latin American diplomat told the author that by the summer of 1989 "President Bush and the Congress will face a stark decision: continue military aid to a government linked to right-wing death squads, or suspend the aid and risk seeing a Marxist guerrilla victory."

Nicaragua provided less of an immediate crisis, but it did present the new administration with difficult choices. As Bush was preparing for his inauguration, there was widespread consensus among senior Democrats and Republicans in Washington that Contra-aid was a dead issue. The Democrats control both chambers in Congress, and the leader of the House of Representatives, Jim Wright, is firmly opposed to any more aid. With delicate negotiations looming over how to tackle the federal budget deficit, the new administration was considered unlikely to want to antagonize the Democratic leadership over the much less important issue of Nicaragua.

Before his inauguration President Bush promised to push for more aid to Contras, but several analysts suggested that the statement was designed to mollify conservatives. "Bush will go through the motions on Contra-aid to keep the conservatives happy," said Bill Goodfellow, director of the Center for International Policy, the main lobbying organization for the Arias peace plan. "He will lose, blame the Democrats in Congress and then forget about it."[15] Indeed, Goodfellow expects the U.S. to grant up to 45,000 visas to the Contras and their dependents and allow them to settle in America as refugees.

After the election the Bush team was already quietly preparing for the demise of the Contras by devising a new policy which it called "Active Containment." According to

Dr. Mark Falcoff, a resident scholar at the American Enterprise Institute who advised the Bush campaign on Central American policy, that means "an attempt to isolate Nicaragua and at the same time (provide) more resources for the other four Central American countries, both military and economic."[16] Allies would be pressured to deny Nicaragua any kind of assistance and to restrict trade. Nicaragua would become an international pariah.

Even that policy implies a level of congressional commitment which Falcoff reckons is dubious. He believes the Bush administration may simply come to the conclusion that Congress no longer views Central America as an area of strategic importance, and so decide to abandon it to benign neglect. As a result there would be little economic or military support for Nicaragua's neighbors and little other substance to the "Active Containment" policy.

At the start of the Bush Administration few analysts expected the new secretary of state, James Baker, to seek a negotiated solution to the Nicaraguan conflict. One who did was Dr. Wayne Smith, a professor of Latin American Studies at Johns Hopkins University and formerly the top U.S. diplomat in Cuba. Dr. Smith argued that Baker is "nothing if not a pragmatist and a realist." As a result he thinks Baker will want to see a resolution of the Central American situation and will lend some support to the Arias peace plan while trying to turn it to America's advantage.[17]

But, as late as March 1989, the Senate had still not ratified Baker's choice for Assistant Secretary of State for Inter-American Affairs. As a result there was a policy vacuum and, once again, the Central American presidents moved to fill the void. On February 14 they agreed to close all the contra bases in Honduras. Although Contra leaders protested that they had not been consulted and vowed to fight on, the move effectively sealed their fate.

In return the Sandinistas promised to release all remaining Guardia prisoners and all those convicted of

Contra activity, an estimated 3,300 people. They also agreed to hold presidential, legislative and municipal elections on February 25, 1990. Under the terms of the pact all political parties would have full, uncensored access to TV, radio and the press and the elections would be monitored at all stages by international observers.

These moves appear to satisfy most of the demands on "democratization" that the Reagan Administration used to justify its support of the Contras. Yet the Sandinistas are confident that they will be able to win the 1990 elections. Indeed they were so confident that they boldly introduced unpopular spending cuts in education and health as well as defense that will result in the layoff of at least 50,000 government employees.

If the Sandinistas comply with the peace plan it seems improbable that the White House will be able to prevent European allies from making fresh loans to Managua. In any case the Central Americans are attempting to revive the regional Common Market, for which Nicaraguan involvement is essential, for geographical reasons if none other: the country sits across the vital trade route between Panama and Costa Rica to the south and Honduras, El Salvador and Guatemala to the north. So Nicaragua's neighbors are unlikely to welcome a U.S. policy of long-term isolation that hamstrings regional trade.

If neither Contra-aid nor "Active Containment" will work, Baker may be tempted to accept bilateral talks with the Sandinistas, in order to guarantee U.S. security concerns. But by the spring of 1989 it was clear that in Washington the urgency was draining from the Nicaraguan debate. Probably because, although the Contras have failed to topple the Sandinistas, they have succeeded in destroying the economy and decimating progressive social programs: in a sense Sandinismo has already been defeated and the U.S. has "won." As Goodfellow said, "Nicaragua now stands as an example of what happens if you dare defy Uncle Sam."

CHRONOLOGY OF DATES IN NICARAGUAN HISTORY

1502	Christopher Columbus "discovers" Nicaragua.
1522	Spanish conquistadores invade, defeat local Chorotec Indians, and establish a colony.
1808	Napoleon Bonaparte seizes Spanish throne, prompting rebellion in Latin America.
1821–38	Central America wins independence from Spain and is annexed by Mexico, then forms a brief regional federation.
1823	President James Monroe announces his Doctrine—Americas no longer open to European colonization.
1838	Nicaragua achieves full independence.
1845–48	U.S. acquires western and Pacific states.
1848	Gold discovered in California.
1850	U.S. and Britain sign Clayton-Bulwer Treaty, agree to jointly operate a Nicaraguan canal.
1851	Cornelius Vanderbilt opens ferry service to California through Nicaragua.
1855–57	William Walker leads filibuster expedition to Nicaragua, declares himself president, is defeated by combined Central American force.
1893	General Zelaya seizes presidency.
1895	Zelaya incorporates Atlantic coast into Nicaragua, expels British.
1898	Spanish-American War marks start of U.S. military intervention in Latin America.
1904	President Theodore Roosevelt announces his Corollary to Monroe Doctrine to justify U.S. "police action" in Latin America.

1909	U.S. backs overthrow of Zelaya, helps establish a regime friendly to U.S.
1912–25	U.S. Marines put down local revolution, occupy Nicaragua.
1926–33	U.S. Marines put down local revolution, occupy Nicaragua, fight nationalist guerrillas led by Gen. Augusto Sandino.
1933	Marines leave, Sandino makes peace, Anastasio Somoza, Sr., appointed commander of national guard.
1934	Sandino assassinated.
1936	Somoza has himself elected president, establishes dictatorial regime.
1939	Somoza received in Washington by President Roosevelt.
1954	Somoza supports CIA-backed overthrow of elected government in Guatemala.
1956	Somoza assassinated, son Luis Somoza succeeds him.
1959	Revolutionaries seize power in Cuba.
1960	Central American Common Market founded.
1961	President Kennedy launches Alliance for Progress.
1961	Sandinista National Liberation Front founded. Nicaragua used as base for Bay of Pigs attack on Cuba.
1963	First FSLN guerrilla operation badly defeated.
1967	Anastasio Somoza, Jr., has himself elected president; Luis Somoza dies of heart attack.
1968	Medellín conference gives birth to Liberation Theology. Somoza launches fierce repression of Sandinistas and peasants in mountains.
1972	Earthquake destroys Managua, 10,000 dead. Start of Somoza's worst corruption, popular discontent starts to grow.
1974	Somoza has himself reelected president. Businessmen unite against him. Sandinistas seize Somoza's friends and relatives as hostages. Somoza pays ransom, releases political prisoners, distributes FSLN propaganda—and unleashes repression.
1978: Jan.	Pedro Joaquin Chamorro assassinated.
Feb.	Insurrection in Masaya, brutally repressed.
Aug.	Sandinistas seize National Palace, Somoza releases prisoners, pays ransom, distributes FSLN propaganda; thousands line streets to cheer guerrillas.
Sep.	FSLN calls for insurrection in major towns, fighting lasts for weeks and is savagely put down.
1979: May	Sandinistas launch final insurrection.
June	Sandinistas promise pluralism, mixed economy, free elections.
July	The Triumph—Somoza goes into exile, Sandinistas take control.
1980: Nov.	Ronald Reagan elected president.
1981: Jan.	Sandinistas support Salvadoran guerrilla "final offensive."

	Mar.	Reagan authorizes covert anti-Sandinista operations.
	May	Argentines start to train Contras.
1982:	Mar.	Contras blow up two bridges; Contra war starts; Sandinistas impose state of emergency.
1983:	Mar.	Pope John Paul II visits Nicaragua.
	Oct.	U.S. invades Grenada.
1984:	Jan.	The CIA mines Nicaraguan harbors.
	Oct.	Congress suspends aid to Contras.
	Nov.	Daniel Ortega elected Nicaraguan president, Ronald Reagan reelected.
1985:	Apr.	Obando elevated to cardinal.
	May	Reagan imposes trade embargo.
	June	Congress resumes funding for Contras.
1986:	Oct.	Sandinistas shoot down Contra supply plane; Iran-Contra affair starts to unravel.
1987:	Aug.	Central American presidents accept Arias peace plan.
1988:	Feb.	Congress rejects new aid for Contras.
	Mar.	Sandinistas and Contras sign ceasefire agreement.

DICTIONARY OF ACRONYMS USED IN THIS BOOK

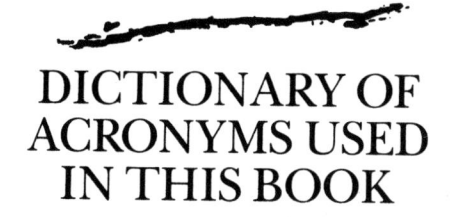

ARDE	Alianza Revolucionaria Democrática	Democratic Revolutionary Alliance (Contra group based in Costa Rica)
CDS	Comité de Defensa Sandinista	Sandinista Defense Committee (pro-FSLN neighborhood groups)
CDN	Coordinadora Democrática Nicaragüense	Nicaraguan Democratic Coordinator (principal domestic conservative anti-Sandinista political alliance)
CEB	Comunidades Eclesiáles de Base	Ecclesiastical Base Communities (progressive bible-study groups)
COSEP	Consejo Superior de la Empresa Privada	High Council of Private Enterprise (private businessmen's principal coordinating body and anti-Sandinista lobby)
CTN	Central de Trabajadores de Nicaragua	Nicaraguan Workers' Federation (Social Christian, affiliated to the CDN)
CUS	Consejo de Unificación Sindical	Council of Trade Union Unification (affiliated to the CDN)

DGSE	Dirección General de Seguridad de Estado	General Directorate of State Security (secret police)
DN	Dirección Nacional	National Directorate (the nine-man FSLN leadership council)
ECLA/CEPAL	Comisión Económica Para America Latina	(United Nations) Economic Commission for Latin America
EEBI	Escuela de Entrenamiento Basico de Infanteria	Basic Infantry Training School (elite national guard unit)
EPS	Ejército Popular Sandinista	Sandinista Popular Army (the national army after 1979)
FAO	Frente Amplio Opositor	Broad Opposition Front (coalition of UDEL, MDN and LOS DOCE)
FDN	Fuerza Democrática Nicaragüense	Nicaraguan Democratic Force (principal Contra alliance of 1981–1985, based in Honduras)
FSLN	Frente Sandinista de Liberación Nacional	Sandinista National Liberation Front (the governing party)
LOS DOCE		The Twelve (group of businessmen, writers, priests, etc. sympathetic to or members of FSLN)
MAP	Movimiento Acción Popular	Popular Action Movement (ultra-left group opposed to the FSLN)
MDN	Movimiento Democrático Nicaragüense	Nicaraguan Democratic Movement (political party led by Alfonso Robelo)
OEA/OAS	Organización de Estados Americanos	Organization of American States. (regional agency established 1948 to promote peace and development)
TPA	Tribunales Populares Antisomocistas	Anti-Somocista Popular Tribunals (special courts to try suspected Contras)
UDEL	Unión Democrática de Liberación	Democratic Liberation Union (anti-Somoza business group)

NOTES

Chapter One
First Encounters

1. For a description of the Gold Rush and its effects on California, see Gordon V. Axon, *The California Gold Rush* (New York: Mason/Charter, 1976).
2. For a description of the hardships of the overland route, see Mary McDougall Gordon, ed., *Overland to California with the Pioneer Line* (California: Stanford University Press, 1983).
3. David I. Folkman, Jr., *The Nicaragua Route* (Salt Lake City: University of Utah Press, 1972), p. 2.
4. For further details of Vanderbilt's life, see Wayne Andrews, *The Vanderbilt Legend* (New York: Harcourt Brace, 1941).
5. *New York Times*, January 5, 1877. Quoted in Folkman, op. cit., p. 53.
6. For more on Walker see Laurence Greene, *The Filibuster* (New York: Bobbs-Merrill, 1937); or Albert Z. Carr, *The World and William Walker* (New York: Macmillan, 1963); or William Walker, *The War in Nicaragua* (Mobile: n.p., 1859).
7. William Walker, op. cit., pp. 273–274.

Chapter Two
A Few Hints for Al Capone

1. Henri Weber, *The Sandinist Revolution* (London: Verso Editions, 1981), p. 1.
2. See Bartolomeo de las Casas, *Devastation of the Indies: A Brief Account* (New York: Continuum, 1974).

3. Thomas W. Walker, *Nicaragua: The Land of Sandino* (Boulder: Westview Press, 1981), p. 11.
4. Harold Norman Denny, *Dollars for Bullets: The Story of American Rule in Nicaragua* (New York: Dial Press, 1929), p. 59. See also Thomas Walker, op. cit., pp. 11–12.
5. For a fuller description see Thomas Walker, op. cit., pp. 1–3.
6. Sergio Ramirez, *La historia viva de Nicaragua* (Mexico: Siglo Veintiuno Editores, 1983), p. 11.
7. Denny, op. cit., p. 16.
8. See Mary W. Williams, *Anglo-American Isthmian Diplomacy, 1815–1915* (New York: Russell and Russell, 1965).
9. Denny, op. cit., p. 16.
10. Denny, op. cit., p. 66.
11. Denny, op. cit., p. 262.
12. For more on the Standard Fruit presence in Nicaragua see Thomas L. Karnes, *Tropical Enterprise, Standard Fruit and Steamship Company in Latin America* (Baton Rouge: Louisiana State University Press, 1978), Chapter 7.
13. Dana G. Munro, *Intervention and Dollar Diplomacy in the Caribbean 1900–1921* (New Jersey: Princeton University Press, 1964), pp. 167–177.
14. Richard Millett, *Guardians of the Dynasty* (New York: Orbis Books, 1977), p. 26.
15. Munro, op. cit., pp. 186–189.
16. Denny, op. cit., p. 1.
17. Denny, op. cit., p. 66.
18. Munro, op. cit., p. 200.
19. Quoted in Jenny Pearce, *Under the Eagle: U.S. Intervention in Central America and the Caribbean* (London: Latin American Bureau, 1982), p. 17.
20. Millett, op. cit., pp. 32–33.
21. Denny, op. cit., p. 367.
22. Carleton Beals, *Latin America: World in Revolution* (London: Abelard-Schuman, 1963), p. 79.
23. Major General Smedley D. Butler, "America's Armed Forces," in *Common Sense*, vol. IV no. 11, New York (November 1935), p. 8.
24. Pearce, op. cit., p. 19.
25. Beals, op. cit., p. 82.
26. Quoted in Beals, op. cit., p. 83.
27. Beals, op. cit., p. 85.

Chapter Three
"That Damned Country"

1. Quoted in Ramirez, op. cit., p. 32.
2. Ibid., p. 26.
3. Shirley Christian, *Nicaragua: Revolution in the Family* (New York: Random House, 1985), p. 9.

4. See Gregorio Selser, *Sandino, General de Hombres Libres* (San José, Costa Rica: Editorial Universitaria Centroamericana, 1980).
5. Quoted in Christian, op. cit., p. 11, and in Carlos Fonseca, *Viva Sandino* (Managua: Editorial Nueva Nicaragua, 1982), p. 50.
6. See Neill Macaulay, *The Sandino Affair* (Chicago: Quadrangle, 1967).
7. George Black, *Triumph of the People: The Sandinista Revolution in Nicaragua* (London: Zed Press, 1981), pp. 21–22.
8. Quoted in Ramirez, op. cit., p. 41.
9. Ibid., p. 35.
10. Black, op. cit., p. 18. Fonseca claims 515 clashes that year: op. cit., p. 56.
11. Ramirez, op. cit., p. 48. See also Millett, op. cit., p. 134.
12. Fonseca, op. cit., p. 69.
13. Augusto Cesar Sandino: Ideario politico (mimeo, n.p.).
14. Millett, op. cit., p. 148.
15. Christian, op. cit., p. 21.
16. Millett, op. cit., pp. 155–163. See also Weber, op. cit., p. 15.

Chapter Four
The Somoza Dynasty and the
Triumph of the Sandinistas

1. Christian, op. cit., p. 24. See also Peter Davis, *Where Is Nicaragua?* (New York: Simon and Schuster, 1987), p. 28.
2. For details on Somoza's accumulation of wealth, see Millett, op. cit., p. 197. Also Weber, op. cit., pp. 16–18. Also Black, op. cit., pp. 34–36.
3. Quoted in Ramirez, op. cit., p. 59.
4. Millett, op. cit., pp. 235–236.
5. Ibid., p. 237.
6. For a discussion of this operation see Davis, op. cit., pp. 19–24.
7. World Bank, *Nicaragua: The Challenge of Reconstruction*, Report No. 3524-NI (Washington, D.C., October 9, 1981), p. 8.
8. Economic Commission for Latin America and the Caribbean (ECLAC), *The Crisis in Central America: Its Origins, Scope and Consequences*, E/CEPAL/G. 1261 (Santiago, Chile: September 15, 1983), p. 13.
9. See Pearce, op. cit.
10. Economic Commission for Latin America and the Caribbean (ECLAC), *Economic Survey: 1978* (New York: United Nations, 1978).
11. For the failure of UDEL to effectively confront Somoza, see Black, op. cit., pp. 100–118.
12. For more on the growing radicalization of the Church in this period, see Michael Dodson and T. S. Montgomery, "The Churches in the Nicaraguan Revolution," in Thomas W. Walker, ed., *Nicaragua in Revolution* (New York: Praeger Publishers, 1982), pp. 161–180.
13. Black, op. cit., pp. 104–106.
14. Ibid., pp. 114–115. See also Christian, op. cit., pp. 51–52.
15. Quoted in Black, op. cit., p. 55. For more on the nature of the Guardia, see Black, op. cit., pp. 46–56. See also Millett, op. cit.

16. Reported to the author by Josefina Ramos, director of the Centro Tutelar de Menores (the Youth Tuition Center), which was founded after 1979 to rehabilitate dozens of disturbed youths who had been recruited by the Guardia.
17. For more on the Sandinista weapons supply operation, see Christian, op. cit., pp. 79–81 and 89–97.
18. The decision to write the letter is commonly called the "Puntarenas Accord." The Reagan administration has alleged failure to carry out the promise as justification for support of the Contras.

Chapter Five
The Honeymoon

1. Interview with the author.
2. For a description of the problems immediately after July 1979, see Michael E. Conroy, "Economic Legacy and Policies: Performance and Critique," in Thomas W. Walker, ed., *Nicaragua: The First Five Years* (New York: Praeger Publishers, 1985).
3. See World Bank, *Nicaragua: The Challenge of Reconstruction,* Report No. 3524-NI (Washington, D.C., October 9, 1981).
4. Ibid.
5. See ECLAC, *The Crisis in Central America*
6. For a discussion of the agricultural legacy, see Joseph Collins, *Nicaragua: What Difference Could a Revolution Make?* (San Francisco: Institute for Food and Development Policy, 1982).
7. Figures from a variety of sources including: World Bank, op. cit.; ECLAC, op. cit.; Fondo Internacional de Desarrollo Agricola (FIDA), *Informe de la Mision Especial de Programacion a Nicaragua* (Rome, 1980); and government statistics.
8. Interview with the author.
9. Interview in *La Nación* (Buenos Aires, Argentina), March 5, 1978, quoted in Black, op. cit., p. 112.
10. *Latin American Political Report,* vol. XIII, no. 17, May 4, 1979, quoted in Black, op. cit., p. 116.
11. Carlos Fonseca, *Bajo la Bandera del Sandinismo* (Managua: Editorial Nueva Nicaragua, 1982), p. 334.
12. Ibid., p. 184. See also Fonseca's essay "Notas sobre la montana y algunos otros temas," pp. 196–215.
13. See Black, op. cit., pp. 334–339.
14. Interview with the author.
15. *Statute on the Rights and Guarantees of Nicaraguans,* August 21, 1979, Section 2, Article 27.
16. For more on this meeting, see *The 72-Hour Document* (Washington: Department of State Publication, Coordinator of Public Diplomacy for Latin America and the Caribbean, 1986). See also Christian, op. cit., pp. 129–130.
17. Quoted in Black, op. cit., p. 185.

18. For descriptions of Sandinista advances in education, health care, housing, etc., see Thomas W. Walker, ed., *Nicaragua in Revolution;* also Thomas W. Walker, ed., *Nicaragua: The First Five Years.*

Chapter Six
The Divorce

1. See Christian, op. cit., p. 140.
2. Ibid., pp. 142–143.
3. For a breakdown of international loans between July 1979 and December 1984, see Daniel Siegel and Tom Spaulding with Peter Kornbluh, *Outcast Among Allies: The International Costs of Reagan's War Against Nicaragua* (Washington: Institute for Policy Studies, 1985).
4. Christian, op. cit., p. 142.
5. Weber, op. cit., p. 59. But for the growing relations between Nicaragua and the Soviet Union, see Theodore Schwab and Harold Sims, "Relations with the Communist States," in Thomas W. Walker, ed., *Nicaragua: The First Five Years,* chapter 22.
6. For more on the development of the armed forces, see Stephen M. Gorman and Thomas W. Walker, "The Armed Forces," in Thomas W. Walker, ed., *Nicaragua: The First Five Years,* chapter 4.
7. Quoted in Weber, op. cit., p. 69.
8. See interview of Borge in "El Poder lo tienen las clases tradicionalmente explotadas," *Cuadernos de Marcha,* No. 1 (January–February 1987), p. 87.
9. But Cardenal had already written to President Reagan as early as December 1980 asking support for an armed force to attack the Sandinistas: see Roy Gutman, *Banana Diplomacy* (New York: Simon and Schuster, 1988), p. 28.
10. Christian, op. cit., pp. 147–150.
11. See Black, op. cit., pp. 255–256.
12. The opposition leaders who have remained in Nicaragua have always maintained that while they sympathize with the objectives of the Contras (removing the FSLN and introducing "western-style democracy"), they disagree with the means. However the Contra leader Adolfo Calero has frequently referred to these internal opponents as "my political wing."
13. See Peter Kornbluh, *Nicaragua: The Price of Intervention* (Washington: Institute for Policy Studies, 1987), p. 19. See also Kornbluh's "The Covert War," in Thomas W. Walker, ed., *Reagan Versus the Sandinistas: The Undeclared War on Nicaragua* (Boulder: Westview Press, 1987).
14. Among them was Adolfo Calero, who would later become the civilian leader of the Contras. For early plotting by businessmen see Gutman, op. cit., chapter 2.
15. Ibid., pp. 35–38. See also comments by David MacMichael, former CIA intelligence analyst, who says no evidence of Sandinista aid to Salvadoran guerrillas was found after February 1981: Testimony of

David MacMichael, International Court of Justice, Nicaragua v. United States of America, April 30, 1985, United Nations, A/40/907, s/17639, November 19, 1985.
16. Kornbluh, op. cit., p. 19.

Chapter Seven
The Birth of the Contras

1. Quoted by Tom Wicker, see "They're Coming Again," *New York Times*, April 2, 1985, p. A27.
2. See Gutman, op. cit.
3. For a description of this incident and a history of the U.S. efforts to create the Contra movement, see Christopher Dickey, *With the Contras* (New York: Simon and Schuster, 1985).
4. Gutman, op. cit., p. 55.
5. Ibid., p. 74, repeated in an interview with the author.
6. This assertion has been widely reported. Adolfo Calero denies it. The CIA has a policy of "neither confirming nor denying" any of its activities, but United States officials have confirmed the information to the author.
7. Figures taken from speech by the Nicaraguan president, Daniel Ortega, on July 19, 1986, at Esteli, Nicaragua.
8. See House of Representatives Permanent Select Committee on Intelligence, *Adverse Report,* March 12, 1986, pp. 5–6.
9. Again the CIA will not publicly confirm or deny these operations. However, they have been confirmed to the author by U.S. officials and widely reported, e.g., in Gutman, op. cit.; Dickey, op. cit.; and Kornbluh, op. cit.
10. See Gutman, op. cit., chapter 8, "Opportunities Missed," pp. 170–185.
11. See Gutman, op. cit., p. 148.

Chapter Eight
Human Rights

1. The incident was widely reported, e.g., in an article by the author in *The Guardian* (London), April 24, 1984.
2. Interview with the author.
3. See Christian, op. cit., p. 133.
4. Figures taken from Amnesty International *Nicaragua: The Human Rights Record,* (London: Amnesty International Publications, 1986) AMR/43/01/86. p. 3, and from Americas Watch, *Human Rights in Nicaragua August 1987 to August 1988* (New York: The Americas Watch Committee, 1988), p. 79.
5. Interview with author.
6. Amnesty International, *Nicaragua: The Human Rights Record,* p. 6.
7. During World War I thousands of Americans were jailed for "antiwar" remarks or for "interfering with recruiting activities." For more

on this see Thomas W. Walker, ed., *Nicaragua: The First Five Years*, pp. 190–192.
8. Amnesty, *Nicaragua: The Human Rights Record*, pp. 1–4.
9. See Amnesty International, *International Report 1986* (London: Amnesty International Publications, 1986).
10. "C.I.A. Tied to Nicaragua Provocations," *New York Times*, September 21, 1988.
11. Following a prison census conducted in February 1988, the International Committee of the Red Cross (ICRC) said there were 3,354 accused Contras and Contra collaborators in jail. Many of these, as Amnesty International acknowledges, have been involved in violent activity against the government. But others, Amnesty believes, have been jailed merely for expressing opposition to the government. See Americas Watch, op. cit., p. 79, for the ICRC numbers.
12. Quoted in Amnesty International, *International Report* 1987.
13. Americas Watch, op. cit., p. 80.
14. Interview with the author.
15. Americas Watch Report, *Human Rights in Nicaragua, 1985–1986* (New York: Americas Watch Committee, March 1986), p. 47.
16. Quoted in John Spicer Nichols, "The Media," in Thomas W. Walker, ed., *Nicaragua: The First Five Years*, p. 187.
17. Ibid.
18. Ibid., pp. 188–190. See also Gutman, op. cit., p. 332.
19. Interview with the author.
20. Figures supplied to the author by the Nicaraguan embassy in Washington, D.C.
21. Amnesty International, *International Report* 1986.
22. Americas Watch, op. cit., pp. 103–125. See also Americas Watch, *Nicaragua: Violations of the Laws of War by Both Sides 1981–1985* (New York: Americas Watch Committee, 1985) and the November 1987 *Supplement* to the same report. See also Reed Brody, *Attacks by the Nicaraguan "Contras" on the Civilian Population of Nicaragua: Report of a Fact-Finding Mission, September 1984–January 1985* (New York: Americas Watch Committee, 1985).
23. See *Report on the Activities of the Permanent Select Committee on Intelligence of the House of Representatives during the Ninety-Eighth Congress* (Washington, D.C.: U.S. Government Printing Office, January 2, 1985).

Chapter Nine
The Economy

1. Author's calculation based on figures in ECLAC, *Economic Survey of Latin America and the Caribbean 1987: Advance Summary* (New York: United Nations, April 12, 1988), LC/G.1511.
2. Kissinger Commission, *Report of the National Bipartisan Commission on Central America* (Washington, D.C.: U.S. Government Printing Office, 1984), p. 30.

3. Figures drawn from the ECLAC annual *Economic Survey of Latin America and the Caribbean, 1979–1987*. See also Michael E. Conroy, op. cit., pp. 221–226. See also Sylvia Maxfield and Richard Stahler-Sholk, "External Constraints," in Thomas W. Walker, ed., *Nicaragua: The First Five Years*, p. 258.
4. World Bank, op. cit., p. ii.
5. See Thomas W. Walker, ed., *Nicaragua: The Land of Sandino*, pp. 47–58.
6. For a good description of the life of a peasant see Joseph Collins, op. cit., chapter 2.
7. Ministerio de Planificacion, *Plan de Reactivacion Economica en Beneficio del Pueblo 1980* (Managua, 1980). p. 114.
8. It took three months for the government to learn that it did not control the 60 percent of the land it originally estimated. See Collins, op. cit., p. 39.
9. See Harris and Vilas, op. cit., pp. 52–53. See also Collins, op. cit., pp. 40–42. See also Thomas W. Walker, ed., *Nicaragua: The First Five Years*, p. 235.
10. Quoted in Collins, op. cit., p. 41.
11. See Conroy, op. cit., p. 234.
12. Interview with author.
13. For specific examples of "economic sabotage" see Collins, op. cit., pp. 45–48.
14. *Latin America Weekly Report* (London: June 10, 1983).
15. Figures published by agriculture minister, Comandante Jaime Wheelock, in "Solo Queremos La Soberania Para Trabajar Por Nuestro Pueblo," *Encuentros* (Managua, February 1982), no. 1, p. 11. See also Joseph R. Thome and David Kaimowitz, "Agrarian Reform," in Thomas W. Walker, ed., *Nicaragua: The First Five Years*.
16. International Bank for Reconstruction and Development (IBRD), *Country Program Paper, Nicaragua* (Discussion Draft) (Washington, D.C., 1982), p. 16, quoted in Richard L. Harris "The Economic Transformation and Industrial Development of Nicaragua" in Harris and Vilas, op. cit., p. 52.
17. See Ivan Garcia, "Estadisticas basicas en el sector agropecuario," *Revolucion y Desarollo* (Managua: MIDINRA, April–June 1984) no. 1.
18. See Conroy, op. cit., pp. 239–240.
19. "Nicaragua Loan Talks Reported," *New York Times*, March 10, 1982. See also Maxfield and Stahler-Sholk, op. cit., pp. 256–262.
20. See my "The U.S. Embargo against Nicaragua—One Year Later," in *Policy Focus* (Washington, D.C.: joint publication of The Center for International Policy and The Overseas Development Council, 1986), no. 3.
21. Economic Commission for Latin America and the Caribbean (ECLAC), *Estudio Economico de America Latina y El Caribe 1987, Nicaragua*, E/CEPAL/LC/L.463/Add.2 (New York: United Nations, July 1988), p. 29.
22. Ibid., p. 27.

Chapter Ten
Holy War

1. Thomas W. Walker, ed., *Nicaragua: The First Five Years*, p. 125.
2. Pastoral letter from the Nicaraguan Episcopate, *Compromiso Cristiano para una Nueva Nicaragua* (Managua, November 17, 1979).
3. See, for example, the motivations of the Christian guerrillas in the 1977 attack on the San Carlos Guardia barracks quoted in Black, op. cit., pp. 102–104. See also Luis Serra, "Ideology, Religion and the Class Struggle in the Nicaraguan Revolution," in Richard Harris and Carlos M. Vilas, eds., *Nicaragua: A Revolution Under Siege* (London: Zed Books, 1985) p. 154.
4. Ibid.
5. See the excellent article by Conor Cruise O'Brien, "God and Man in Nicaragua," in *The Atlantic Monthly*, vol. 258, no. 2 (August 1986), pp. 50–72.
6. Fonseca, *Bajo la Bandera del Sandinismo*, pp. 333–335.
7. From a document used at the Sandinistas' first Assembly of Cadres, quoted in Black, op. cit., p. 321.
8. Monsignor Bosco Vivas, auxiliary bishop of Managua, quoted in Christian, op. cit., p. 221.
9. O'Brien (op. cit.) is especially helpful on this subject.
10. It was published in full in *La Prensa*, September 1, 1983.
11. Quoted in O'Brien, op. cit., p. 51.
12. Its first publication was written by a former editor of *La Prensa*, Humberto Belli, *Nicaragua: Christians under Fire* (San José, Costa Rica: Instituto Puebla, n.d.) The CIA connection was explained by Chamorro in an interview with the author, and has been cited in other publications.
13. President Ronald Reagan's radio address to the nation, December 14, 1985.
14. For American contributions and political links to the Nicaraguan church hierarchy see Betsy Cohn and Patricia Hynds, "The Manipulation of the Religion Issue," in Thomas W. Walker, ed., *Reagan Versus the Sandinistas*.
15. Interviews with the author.

Chapter Eleven
From Reagan to Bush

1. "Aplastar La Contrarevolución" speech reprinted in *Barricada*, Managua, August 24, 1984.
2. See Christian, op. cit., p. 299.
3. Interview with the author.
4. See criticisms in Weber, op. cit., p. 111.
5. Gutman, op. cit., pp. 233–234.
6. President Reagan's speech, July 19, 1984.
7. Gutman, op. cit., chapter 11, "Divided Counsel," pp. 232–255.

8. Rappaccioli repeated the comment to the *Washington Post,* and Cruz made a similar remark to NBC correspondent Fred Francis, before he left Washington.
9. Interviews with the author.
10. Gutman, op. cit., p. 244–246.
11. Quoted in Siegel, Spaulding and Kornbluh, op. cit., p. 5. See also LASA, *The Electoral Process in Nicaragua: Domestic and International Influences* (Austin, Texas: The Latin American Studies Association, 1984).
12. Nicaraguan and foreign officials interviewed by author.
13. Gutman, p. 317.
14. Reported to the author by several Central American diplomats.
15. Interview with the author.
16. Interview with the author.
17. Interview with the author.

FOR FURTHER READING

Cabezas, Omar. *Fire from the Mountain.* New York: Crown. 1985

Cheney, Glen Alan. *Revolution in Central America.* New York: Watts. 1984.

Christian, Shirley. *Nicaragua: Revolution in the Family.* New York: Random House. 1985.

Cockburn, Leslie. *Out of Control: The Story of the Reagan Administration's Secret War in Nicaragua.* New York: Atlantic Monthly Press. 1987.

Davis, Peter. *Where Is Nicaragua?* New York: Simon and Schuster. 1987.

Dickey, Christopher. *With the Contras.* New York: Simon and Schuster. 1987.

Gelman, Rita Golden. *Inside Nicaragua: Young People's Dreams and Fears.* New York: Watts. 1988.

Gutman, Roy. *Banana Diplomacy.* New York: Simon and Schuster. 1988.

Tessendorf, K. C. *Uncle Sam in Nicaragua.* New York: Atheneum. 1987.

Walker, Thomas W., ed. *Nicaragua: The First Five Years.* New York: Praeger. 1985.

Walker, Thomas W., ed. *Nicaragua in Revolution.* New York: Praeger. 1982.

INDEX

Page numbers in *italics* refer to illustrations.

Acronyms used in book, 175–176
Aguero, Fernando, 54, 56
Americas Watch, 117, 120–122
Amnesty International, 63, 114–115, 117, 121
Arguello, Leonardo, 48–49, 52

Bautista, Juan Sacasa, 32–33, 41–42, 44, 46–48
Borge, Tomas, 58, 63, 68, 70, 78; basic rights, 85, 90, 111–112, 122, 147, 155
Britain, 13, 19, 23, 26, 40, 108; Diplock courts, 118
Broad Opposition Front (FAO), 65–66, 68–70
Bryan-Chamorro Treaty, 31, 45
Burgeses, 75–78, 81–82, 91–92, 96, 115, 130

Canal, Nicaraguan proposed, 13, *20–21*, 26, 31
Cardenal, Ernesto, 142–*143*, 146
Cardenal, Fernando, 142, 147, 151
Cardenal, José F., 92, 96
Carrion, Luis, 85, 146
Carter, Jimmy, 64–65, 68–70, 74, 88–90, 96–97
Castro, F., 54, 59–60, 94, 146
Catholic Church, 58, 62–64, 141–153, 164, 168
Central Intelligence Agency (CIA), 68, 74, 83, 87, 90; against Sandinistas, 97–98, 101–102, 104–108, 115, 120–122, 136–137; Contras funded, 150–152, 163–167
Chamorro, Jaime, *119*, 121
Chamorro, Pedro, 64, 93, 120
Chamorro, Violeta, 69, 70, 93
Chorotec Indians, 14–15, 17, 22, 39–40, 65
Chronology of dates, 172–174
Clayton-Bulwer Treaty, 21
Communism, 45–46, 53, 58, 60–61, 68; advisors, 70, 74, 84–88, 99–100, 109; Nicaraguan party, 77, 160–163

/ 188 /

Conservatives, 16, 18, 26, 29, 37, 44; Chamorro, 32, 47; democratic, 160–162; recruitment, 80; trade, 22
Contras, 121–122, 153, 159–171; invasion, 104–105, 110, 113, 116–117; and U.S., 98, 100–101, 111, 120, 150
Coordinadora Democrática Nicaragüense (CDN), 157, 159–160
COSEP, 81, 83–84, 91–96, 129–133, 157–159
Costa Rica, 13, 52–53, 104, 166; FSLN, 68–69, 76, 102
Council of State, 81, 91–92, 95
Cruz, Arturo, 76, 93, 103, 157–158, 159–160
Cuba, 25–27, 29, 74, 86–88, 106; and FSLN, 59, 62–63, 66, 69, 82

Democratic Liberation Union (UDEL), 62, 64–65
Díaz, Adolfo, 26–29, 31–33, 36–37
Dirección General de Seguridad de Estado (DGSE), 114, 116
Dirección Naçional (DN), 68, 78, 81, 84–87, 94
Dominican Republic, 25, 29, 54, 61

Earthquake (1972), 56–58, *57*, 73
Economy, 39, 44, 47, 61–62, 123–140, *132*
Elections, 52–56, 62, 65, 94, 154–162, *161;* 1985, 106; 1987, 167, 170–171
El Salvador, 13, 26, 40, 61, 96–98, 111; elections, 18, 157, 162; nationalized trade, 130; religious freedom, 152; Sandinista aid, 102, 136; and U.S., 166
Enders, Thomas, 99, 102, 136
Espino Negro Pact, 33, 36, 73
Exports, 15–17, 19, 21–24, 72, 126–130; modern, 39–40, 45, 51, 59–62, 135–139

Fonseca, Carlos, 58, 63, 76, 147
France, 16, 19–20, 90, 108

Geography, 18–19, 21–22
"Group of Twelve," 64–65, 68
Guardia Nacional, 34, 37, 40–60, *50,* 63–66, 69–70; remnants, 72, 95, 100–102, 112, 170–171; training, 90, 107
Guatemala, 13–14, 23, 61, 96–97, 102, 111; and the CIA, 53, 74, 83; religious freedom in, 152

Honduras, 13, 18, 22–27, 29, 47–48; Contras, 70, 101–102, 162–163, 170; outside influences, 97, 102, 111
Human rights groups, 116, 121

Iran-Contra affair, 99, 101, 108–109, *117,* 165–170

Junta, 69–71, 75–78, 83–85, 90–93, 156; censorship, 95, 112–114, 118

Liberals, 16, 44, 47–49, 80, 160–162

Mexico, 10–12, 16, 19–20, 33, 36; FSLN and, 76, 87; Tacho, 52
Miskito Indians, 19, 133

Nicaraguan Democratic Force (FDN), 101–104, *103,* 107–108, 121, 163
Nicaraguan Democratic Movement (MDN), 65, 76, 80, 91–92, 95, 103
Nicaraguan Socialist Party, 88, 91, 145, 160–162

Obando y Bravo, M., 74, 144–145, 147–153, *148,* 157, 168
Organization of American States (OAS), 68–70

Ortega, Daniel, 68, 85, 88–89, 94, *142*, 163; Cuban advice, 106; public meetings, 156; synthesis of ideologies, 147
Ortega, Humberto, 68, 80, 85–86, 90, 94; and lecture on democracy, 155

Pallais, Luis Debayle, 101
Panama, 25, 27, 29, 66, 87; canal, 7, 19, 21, 26, 31, 88
Pastora, Eden, 66, 69, 103–104, 163
Popular Action Movement (MAP), 77, 160–162
Popular Social Christians, 91, 160–162
La Prensa, 64, 93–95, 118–121, *119*, 164; reopened, 168
La Purisima, 141, *142*

Reagan, Ronald, 95–101, 105, 108–115, 120–126, *124;* aid cut, 136; approval of CIA help to Contras, 117, 154, 156–157, 162–163, 165–166, 171; elections, 162, 171; El Salvador, 130; embargo, 134, 137; religious freedom, 141, 151–152
Robelo, A., 65, 69, 74–76, 81, 86, 163; FSLN, 91–96, 103–104

Sandinista Defense Committees (CDCs), 78–80, 91, 155
Sandinista National Liberation Front (FSLN), 58–59, 62–76, 67, 78–87, *79;* Arias peace plan, 167–170; CIA, 97, 102–106, 120–121; Contra invasion, 104–105, 107–108, 113–116, 162–163; criticism, 91–93, 111; crops, 139–140; draft, 150–151; draft treaty, 106; elections, 155–156, 160–162; reforms, 83–84, 101, 111–112, 122, 126–133, 140; religion, 141–153; Triumph, 70–76; and U.S., 90, 99–100, 120, 164
Sandinista Popular Army (EPS), 80, 82, 90, 92, *164*
Sandino, Augusto, 33–47, *35*, 59–60
Social Christian Party, 54, 78, 80, 91–92
Somoza, Anastasio Debayle (Tachito), 53–60, *55*, 62–73, 81, 101, 145
Somoza, Anastasio Garcia (Tacho), 42–53, *43*, 55, 67
Somoza, Anastasio Portacarrero (EL Chiguin), 65–66
Somoza, Luis, 53–56
Soviet Union, 84, 87–90, 94, 97–100, 137, 163
Spain, 14–17, 19–21, 25
Stimson, H., 21, 33–35, 40, 42

Tribunales populares antisomocistas (TPAs), 112, 116–*117*, 118, 120, 168

U.N. Economic Commission for Latin America, 60, 126
United States, 13, 25–*30*, 33, 37–41, 45, 115; President Bush, 168–171; President Coolidge, 32–34; presidential intervention, 12–13, 20–21, 24–26, 29, 41–42, 49–53; President Kennedy, 60–62

Vanderbilt, C., 8, 10, 13

Walker, William, 8–14, *11*, 17–18, 73

Zelaya, José S., 22–23, 26–27

ASHEVILLE-BUNCOMBE
TECHNICAL COMMUNITY COLLEGE

3 3312 00034 2527